Hitler, Chamberlain and appeasement

Frank McDonough

CAMBRIDGE
UNIVERSITY PRESS

For Ann

CAMBRIDGE UNIVERSITY PRESS
Cambridge, New York, Melbourne, Madrid, Cape Town, Singapore, São Paulo, Delhi

Cambridge University Press
The Edinburgh Building, Cambridge CB2 8RU, UK

www.cambridge.org
Information on this title: www.cambridge.org/9780521000482

© Cambridge University Press 2002

This publication is in copyright. Subject to statutory exception
and to the provisions of relevant collective licensing agreements,
no reproduction of any part may take place without the written
permission of Cambridge University Press.

First published 2002
6th printing 2008

Printed in the United Kingdom at the University Press, Cambridge

A catalogue record for this publication is available from the British Library

ISBN 978-0-521-00048-2 paperback

Text design by Newton Harris Design Partnership

Map illustrations by Kathy Baxendale

ACKNOWLEDGEMENTS
Cover, © CORBIS; 45, 61, 70, reproduced with permission of Punch Ltd;
51, Hulton/Archive; 53, David Low/Evening Standard 30.9.38, Centre for the
Study of Cartoons and Caricature; 72, John Frost Newspapers.

Picture research by Sandie Huskinson-Rolfe of PHOTOSEEKERS.

The cover illustration shows Chamberlain and Hitler at the 1938 Munich
conference at which Chamberlain agreed to allow Nazi Germany to annex the
Sudetenland.

Contents

Contents

Introduction

In spite of the many viewpoints which have been put forward to explain the outbreak of the Second World War, two interpretations dominate the historical debate.

The first view suggests that the key reason for the start of the war was Adolf Hitler's cold-blooded desire for European expansion. This interpretation is enshrined in the final judgement at the famous Nuremberg trials of the leading (living) Nazis, which were held shortly after the end of hostilities. Although many new details have emerged concerning the conduct of German foreign policy under the Nazi regime, the central view of Hitler as a uniquely evil and brutal dictator plotting and scheming a war of conquest for *Lebensraum* (living space) in the east from the moment he came to power until the outbreak of war has not been substantially modified or revised.

The second key explanation of the outbreak of the Second World War concentrates on the role played by Neville Chamberlain and the policy of appeasement. This policy did prevent a major European war starting in 1938 through the signing of the Munich agreement, but it ended in humiliating failure when Germany attacked Poland in September 1939. In the popular mind, appeasement has been viewed (and is still generally viewed by world leaders) as a totally disreputable policy of shameful surrender which 'sacrifices principles' in order to 'buy off' a potential or actual aggressor. However, among historians, using more objective methods, the original view of Chamberlain as an incompetent leader and appeasement as a morally bankrupt policy doomed to failure has undergone a quite remarkable transformation. It has, indeed, now become commonplace for 'revisionist historians' to portray Chamberlain not as a weak and ineffective leader but as a complex and able politician with a clear-sighted approach to a foreign policy, who sought peace while at the same time preparing for war.

The main aim of this book is to examine the central roles played by Hitler and Chamberlain in the events which led to the outbreak of the Second World War. The book seeks to adopt a balanced approach to the subject, but does not flinch from giving fresh insights or offering critical assessment when it is deemed necessary. The major focus of the study is, of course, on Anglo-German relations from 1918 to 1939, with particular attention paid to the key events from 1937 to 1939, when Hitler pursued a bold and aggressive foreign policy, while Chamberlain strove energetically to satisfy the 'legitimate' demands made by Hitler, in the hope that this would prevent war.

Introduction

The book begins with a brief survey of the key events in Anglo-German relations from 1918 to 1933. In Chapter 2, the foreign-policy ideas, aims and actions of Adolf Hitler in the period from 1933 to 1937 are explored. Chapter 3 examines the factors which help to explain why appeasement became the policy adopted by the British government to deal with the growing tension in European relations during the 1930s. Chapters 4 and 5 concentrate on events in Anglo-German relations from 1937 to 1939. The book concludes with an extensive analysis of the changing nature of the debate over the roles of Hitler and Chamberlain in the origins of the Second World War.

1

Anglo-German relations, 1918–33

The legacies of the First World War

During the First World War, Britain and Germany were bitter enemies. British wartime propaganda even went as far as depicting German soldiers eating babies in Belgium. When the war ended in 1918, antagonism against German militarism still remained powerful among the British public and in the popular press.

The British reaction to victory

Though Britain emerged victorious from the 'Great War', the economic costs had been crippling. The world export trade, on which British prosperity depended, collapsed. The British government was also saddled with a glut of war debts. Unemployment was rising in the industrial regions, while rural areas were suffering from a severe fall in agricultural prices.

In such a gloomy atmosphere, the popular press cry of 'Make Germany pay' accurately reflected British public opinion. Public demands for retribution against Germany were also voiced in France, Italy and Belgium. It was very difficult to imagine that Germany would be treated leniently when the leading powers assembled in Versailles in the early months of 1919 to hammer out a peace settlement.

The German reaction to defeat

In Germany, meanwhile, there was very little appreciation of the scale of the German military debacle. Most of the population believed that because the German government had signed an armistice at the end of the war, this entitled Germany to a lenient peace settlement. Many ex-soldiers, egged on by the nationalist right, put out a myth that the German army had not been defeated in battle by the superior military prowess of its opponents, but had been 'stabbed in the back' by socialists and liberals, who had undermined the war effort. It was possible to believe in this myth because the war had not been fought on German soil, and Germany had not been invaded or occupied by enemy troops.

The major aims of British foreign policy after the war

The major aim of British foreign policy in the aftermath of the First World War was to promote European co-operation. In July 1921, Winston Churchill, then colonial secretary, claimed the chief aim of British foreign policy was the

3

'appeasement of the fearful hatreds and antagonisms which exist in Europe'. However, the British government realised that Europe would be secure only when Germany became fully reconciled to its new diminished role in the new international order. As a result, foreign-policy makers thought that Britain should adopt a conciliatory middle position in post-war European affairs, attempting to arbitrate between the powerful French desire to obtain security against a possible German military revival and the German desire to be treated with fairness.

A large number of leading economic experts in Britain, most notably John Maynard Keynes, the brilliant young Cambridge economist, argued that German economic revival was extremely important to the recovery of Britain's export trade in Europe, as Germany had been the largest European market for British goods before the First World War.

The Paris peace conference

The British attitude towards the 'German problem' at the Paris peace conference

The British delegation at the Paris peace conference, led by David Lloyd George, the prime minister, took a balanced view of the 'German problem'. Lloyd George did want military restrictions to be placed on German armed forces and financial compensation to be levied against Germany to defray the costs of the war. He did not, though, favour a totally punitive and vindictive territorial and financial settlement. In fact, he believed a vengeful peace settlement, which left the German economy crippled, would only encourage the emergence of a German government hell bent on revenge, thereby opening up the very real prospect of a Second World War taking place.

There were several reasons why Britain could afford to adopt a lenient attitude towards Germany. The defeat of Germany had achieved Britain's chief wartime objective, namely the destruction of German military power. More importantly, the German threat to Britain's mastery of the seas had ended. Germany no longer posed a major threat to the sea lanes and the trade of the British empire. In such circumstances, the British government wanted to retreat from direct involvement in sorting out difficult problems on the European continent.

The French desire for security

The vexed issue of German military power, viewed as the chief cause of the First World War, became the dominant issue in the deliberations of the peacemakers. The French delegation, led by Georges Clemenceau, the French prime minister, laid emphasis on how close Germany had come to victory on the battlefield and suggested that Germany had the economic potential to engineer a military revival at a future date. To prevent this, the French wanted watertight restrictions on the German armed forces, combined with substantial financial compensation for the extensive devastation caused by the German armed forces on French territory.

The demand for national self-determination

The smaller states of eastern Europe demanded national self-determination. To placate these demands, the Paris peace settlement created two new states, Czechoslovakia and Yugoslavia, composed of a wide variety of ethnic groups, and restored the independence of Poland for the first time in over 150 years. These changes were made possible by means of the division of the former territories of the Austro-Hungarian and Turkish empires and by allocating land from the former German empire. Eastern Europe, however, became even more unstable and ethnically divided than ever before. As Lloyd George commented: 'I cannot imagine any greater cause of future war than that the German people, who have proved themselves one of the most powerful and vigorous races in the world, should be surrounded by a number of small states, many of them consisting of peoples who have never previously set up a stable government for themselves'. The British government was very firmly opposed to any commitment to uphold the security of the newly created small states of eastern Europe. It was left to France (a nation which could not defend them) to support these small states by signing a number of diplomatic pacts of mutual assistance with Poland (1921), Czechoslovakia (1924), Romania (1926) and Yugoslavia (1927).

A further doubt over the security of eastern Europe revolved around the communist Soviet Union (modern-day Russia). Russia had been a close ally of France before 1914, but the Soviet Union remained in political and diplomatic isolation for most of the inter-war period. There was great uncertainty about what the foreign-policy aims of the new communist regime would be. Many British policy makers feared a spread of communist ideas in Europe, which would threaten British trading interests and the stability of eastern Europe.

One of the major problems with the peace settlement was its failure to create a viable balance of power in eastern Europe. As a result, if Germany could regain its military and economic strength, it was in a much stronger position to pose a potent threat to eastern Europe than it had been in before 1914. In such circumstances, it was quite clear that German nationalists looked to eastern Europe as an arena for future German expansion. However, the determined French effort to point out the consequences of a possible German revival was not listened to very seriously by either the British or the US government.

The Treaty of Versailles

The Treaty of Versailles, agreed after six months of discussion, was designed to solve the 'German problem' once and for all. The German delegation, under protest, signed the treaty on 28 June 1919. Under the terms of Versailles, the German army, previously the strongest and most well equipped in Europe, was reduced to a mere 100,000 troops, with conscription prohibited. The German navy, the second largest in Europe before 1914, was slimmed down to a coastal defence force, composed of 36 vessels. In addition, the German armed forces were not allowed to possess tanks, submarines, battleships or aircraft.

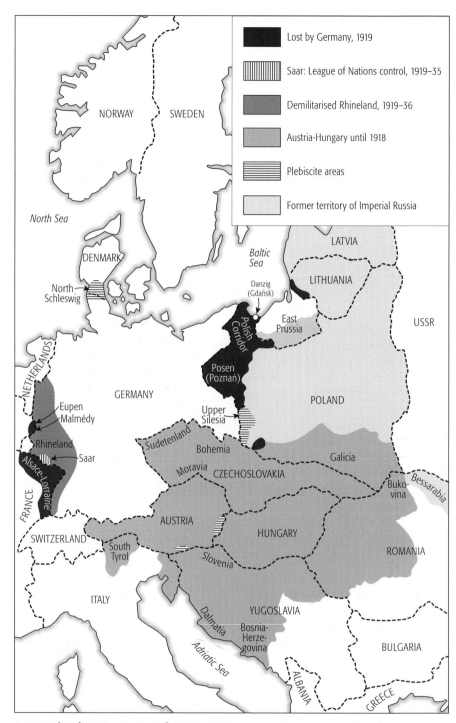

Lost by Germany, 1919

Saar: League of Nations control, 1919–35

Demilitarised Rhineland, 1919–36

Austria-Hungary until 1918

Plebiscite areas

Former territory of Imperial Russia

NORWAY

SWEDEN

North Sea

DENMARK

Baltic Sea

LATVIA

LITHUANIA

North Schleswig

Danzig (Gdańsk)

East Prussia

USSR

NETHERLANDS

GERMANY

Polish Corridor

Posen (Poznań)

POLAND

Eupen Malmédy

Upper Silesia

Rhineland

Saar

Sudetenland

Bohemia

Galicia

Bukovina

Bessarabia

Alsace-Lorraine

Moravia

CZECHOSLOVAKIA

FRANCE

SWITZERLAND

AUSTRIA

HUNGARY

ROMANIA

South Tyrol

Slovenia

ITALY

YUGOSLAVIA

Dalmatia

Bosnia-Herze-govina

BULGARIA

Adriatic Sea

ALBANIA

GREECE

Europe after the Paris peace settlement, 1919.

Germany also lost 13 per cent of its former national territory under the terms of the treaty. In western Europe, Alsace-Lorraine was returned to France, the Rhineland was designated a demilitarised zone and the Saar coalmining region was placed under the control of the newly formed League of Nations. In central Europe, Germany lost the Baltic port of Danzig (modern-day Gdańsk), which was turned into a 'free city', nominally under League of Nations jurisdiction but linked by a customs union to the new independent Polish state, which was also awarded Upper Silesia, a former major German industrial centre. Of all these territorial losses, the most greatly disliked throughout Germany were the loss of Danzig and especially the creation of the so-called 'Polish Corridor', because it separated historic East Prussia, the birthplace of German nationalism, from the remainder of German territory.

To further restrict the spread of German nationalism, any union between Austria and Germany was strictly forbidden even though many economic experts – and nationalists – in both countries agreed that the only viable way for a severely weakened Austria to prosper in the post-war world was through its incorporation within Germany. Outside Europe, every former German colony was confiscated and placed under the supervisory 'mandate' of Britain, France or Italy. On the financial side, all German foreign assets were seized. Even worse, the German government was required to pay compensation (known as reparations) to the victorious Allies for the damage, death and disability caused by the war. The final figure (agreed in 1921) was put at the then enormous figure of £6.6 billion (at 1919 values). This was to be paid in annual instalments by the German government until 1983. Under Article 231 (dubbed 'the war guilt clause'), Germany was obliged to accept full responsibility for starting the First World War. Finally, the Allies insisted that Germany uphold a democratic constitution and free elections.

Not surprisingly, the terms of the Treaty of Versailles were greeted with utter disbelief and anger throughout Germany. The German leaders who signed the so-called 'slave treaty' were branded by nationalists as 'the criminals of 1919'. It is, of course, quite legitimate to point out that the loss of 13 per cent of the nation's territory was less harsh than the loss the French government had suffered at the Congress of Vienna in 1814–15, which had followed the French defeat in the Napoleonic Wars. It is also worth adding that the territorial losses inflicted on Germany were much less punitive than those Germany itself imposed on Russia under the Treaty of Brest-Litovsk (1918).

Even the compensation demanded of Germany in the form of reparations payments was affordable, if the Germans had shown any willingness to pay them. It can even be suggested that reparations were quite a legitimate demand. After all, most German territory and industrial machinery lay undamaged, while most of the productive areas of France had suffered severe damage or destruction in the unprovoked German assault on that nation at the outset of the conflict.

However, this sober analysis of the Treaty of Versailles is of less significance than the psychological impact of the treaty on the German people. Versailles became the most hated word in Germany after 1919. The issue of whether the nation had the capacity to pay reparations (which it did) was hardly ever discussed in a rational manner. In fact, the strong reaction against Versailles both foretold the future and explained a current reality. The great majority of Germans refused to accept the result of the First World War. As a consequence, the Treaty of Versailles was not a final settlement of that conflict. At some future date, a German government, of a nationalist tinge, would definitely seek to revise the treaty. It is, indeed, extremely unlikely that the German government and people would ever have accepted any peace treaty that was put before them by the Allies, except the most lenient one imaginable.

The real problem with the Treaty of Versailles was twofold. Firstly, it was not an effective diplomatic agreement, because its enforcement relied heavily on continuing German compliance, which was not guaranteed. Secondly, it was not a sufficiently secure deterrent against a German military revival. In the absence of any real machinery and willingness to enforce its terms, the treaty was just a piece of paper, capable of being challenged and revised by Germany.

The League of Nations

The Paris peace conference also gave birth to the League of Nations, based in Geneva, which was designed to establish a completely new framework for conducting relations between nations. The League had the power (on paper) to impose economic sanctions and to threaten an invading power with the prospect of all League members acting collectively (known as collective security) to remove the aggressor by military force. The burden of maintaining peace in the world was to be the shared responsibility of all nations.

There was great initial faith among the British public in the ability of the League to prevent a future war. It was not fully appreciated that the League could act as an effective peacekeeper only if it retained the support of the majority of world powers.

The Allies' different approaches to the Treaty of Versailles

In the early 1920s, the French government did attempt to uphold the Treaty of Versailles. However, the British government showed a willingness to revise it in Germany's favour. Indeed, the powerful German belief in the harshness of the Treaty of Versailles was soon generally accepted by British policy makers. The US Senate further strengthened the German case for revision by refusing to ratify the treaty because of its alleged harshness.

In fact, the more energetically the French government attempted to enforce the terms of the treaty, the less support it received from the British. In the immediate aftermath of the First World War, the British government became concerned that France, now the most dominant military power in Europe, might attempt to bully Germany. As a result, it was unwilling to underwrite French military power in Europe and refused to renew its wartime alliance with France. The Foreign Office quite optimistically predicted (in 1926) that a German military revival was extremely unlikely, at least until the 1960s or 1970s. The key aim of British policy after the First World War was to avoid encouraging a spirit of revenge to develop in Germany, but instead to offer the hand of friendship towards a former defeated enemy.

The German desire to revise Versailles

It was, in fact, widely accepted in Britain that the German government would strive to revise the Treaty of Versailles and, provided legitimate German grievances were being appeased, the British government would not oppose such revision. Hence, the British policy of appeasing German grievances was already a factor in British policy on the 'German problem' in the 1920s. Lloyd George believed that appeasement was a vital antidote to French antagonism towards Germany. Yet this type of appeasement was designed to persuade the German government to accept its new diminished military position in Europe. It was also undertaken from a position of military strength.

The reparations problem

The first major issue of dispute between the Allies and Germany over the Treaty of Versailles was the payment of financial compensation (reparations). Germany had emerged from the war with a new democratic government (which was not popular among large sections of the population) and quite staggering problems. The German Weimar Republic was born in a climate of defeat, humiliation and disorder. Instability, with no single party commanding a majority in parliament (the Reichstag), was a permanent feature of political life. There was bitter fighting between left-wing and right-wing groups out on the streets. To make matters worse, Germany was beset by deep economic problems. Most Germans were inclined to blame these on the demands made by the Allies for reparations. From 1918 to 1923, the German mark fell dramatically in value in relation to the other major currencies (the pound, the dollar and the franc), pushing inflation (the price of goods) ever upwards. In 1923, for example, one pre-1914 gold mark was worth 2,500 marks. The German government blamed the 'great inflation' on the demand made by the Allies for the payment of reparations.

The German battle to resist the full payment of reparations became the most dominant and bitter issue in European relations during the 1920s. The French government viewed reparations payments as vital to the recovery of the French economy. The German government, supported by all sides of the political spectrum, was opposed to repayment. A bitter clash between France and Germany over the payment of reparations was inevitable. The British government decided to adopt a middle position in this dispute, but sympathised with, and generally came to support, the German demand for a reduction in payments. The result was constant Anglo-French disharmony over how to deal with Germany. As Lord Curzon, the foreign secretary, put it: 'If the French and ourselves permanently fall out, I see no prospect of the recovery of Europe or the pacification of the world'.

On 9 January 1923, the French government, led by Raymond Poincaré, frustrated with the continual default on reparations payments by the German government and ignoring British calls for restraint, decided to occupy the Ruhr in a last desperate attempt to force the German government to pay up. The German government adopted a policy of 'passive resistance' to the occupation.

The Dawes Plan

The occupation of the Ruhr (which lasted for the first nine months of 1923) was a failure but also a turning point in European relations. The whole sorry episode showed that the French government, acting without British support, could not force Germany to pay reparations. At the same time, the German government, fully aware of its current, unfamiliar, military weakness, accepted, albeit reluctantly, that continual non-payment was unlikely to gain a reduction in reparations payments.

In order to find a workable solution, Germany and France agreed to US mediation over the problem. In April 1924, an Allied committee on reparations, chaired by Charles G. Dawes, a leading US banker, examined Germany's ability to meet its payments. The 'Dawes Plan', ratified at the London reparations conference in August 1924, was, in fact, a major act of appeasement towards German grievances over the Treaty of Versailles. The agreement was extremely favourable towards Germany. It offered the German government a very substantial US bank loan to meet its repayments, and further substantial financial aid (in the form of loans) to support the introduction of a new German mark (the Rentenmark), based on land and industrial property. These measures helped to end the era of hyperinflation in Germany. The French government, in a further act of reconciliation, promised not to use military force to get Germany to pay reparations ever again.

The Dawes Plan took the heat out of the reparations issue. Its major flaw, however, was its dependence on US financial support. In fact, the German government agreed to pay the reduced annual repayments of reparations decided under the Dawes Plan only with the help of borrowed money from US banks. In essence, Germany was borrowing from one former enemy (the USA) to pay four other former enemies (France, Britain, Italy and Belgium). As a result, the Dawes Plan provided only a breathing space in the reparations battle, not a permanent solution. The recovery of the German economy was dependent on the continued ability of US banks to provide short-term loans to Germany.

The Locarno treaties

The conciliatory diplomatic stance of the German government during the negotiation of the Dawes Plan was greatly influenced by Gustav Stresemann, the German foreign minister (1923–29). Stresemann believed the best way for Germany to gain concessions from the Allies while Germany remained in a severely weakened militarily position was to adopt a policy of co-operation. The most significant achievement of Stresemann's conciliatory approach to European relations was the Locarno treaties, signed by Germany, Britain, Belgium, France and Italy in October 1925. These agreements were viewed by the British government as a vital means of easing Franco-German antagonism. Sir Austen Chamberlain, the British foreign secretary, though opposed to signing a formal alliance with France, was prepared to commit Britain to guarantee France and Belgium against possible German aggression in western Europe.

Under the terms of Locarno, Germany accepted the territorial arrangements outlined in the Treaty of Versailles in relation to western Europe, most notably the demilitarisation of the Rhineland and the loss of Alsace-Lorraine. In return, the western Allies (France, Britain and Italy) agreed to end their military occupation of the Rhineland (which took place in 1930) and curtailed their inspection of the German armed forces. In response, Germany agreed to join the League of Nations. The three leading signatories of the Locarno treaties – Stresemann, Chamberlain and Aristide Briand (the French foreign minister) – were all subsequently awarded the prestigious Nobel Peace Prize in recognition of their efforts.

To most contemporary observers, the Locarno treaties, which treated Germany as an equal partner in European affairs, laid the basis for a lasting peace in Europe. The acrimonious Franco-German quarrel which had blighted post-war European relations appeared to have been resolved. The new mood of optimism which followed Locarno (dubbed 'the Locarno honeymoon') greatly encouraged the signing of the Kellogg–Briand pact of August 1928 (Frank Kellogg was the US secretary of state). Under the Kellogg–Briand pact, 15 nations (including Germany, Britain, France and the USA) renounced war as a legitimate weapon for a nation state (and they had been joined by many more nations by the end of the 1920s).

What were the aims of Stresemann's foreign policy?

The sudden change in German foreign policy in the mid-1920s from confrontation towards conciliation has been the subject of much discussion among historians. Most of this debate has centred on the aims of German foreign policy under Stresemann. It is certainly true that Stresemann did seek peaceful relations with the victorious Allies and he supported the integration of Germany into the system of security in western Europe laid out in the Locarno treaties. However, the German government gave no promise that it accepted its eastern borders. On the contrary, Stresemann made no secret of his deep hostility towards these territorial settlements. As a result, the Locarno treaties left open the possibility of Germany pursuing claims to territory in eastern Europe at a later date. A further glaring weakness of the Locarno security system was that it completely ignored the Soviet Union, the most powerful country in eastern Europe. As a result, there was no real security system for that region, which was left in a state of uncertainty.

In recent studies, historians have cast doubt over whether Stresemann's conciliatory diplomacy was genuine at all. In public, Stresemann was a 'good European' and a peacekeeper, but in private he remained a staunch German nationalist, who wanted to end reparations, remove all occupied troops from

Germany and obtain a revision of the eastern European territorial arrangements set out in the Treaty of Versailles at a more convenient future date.

On the other hand, it must be emphasised that Stresemann believed Germany could revise the Treaty of Versailles by means of peaceful negotiation and skilful diplomacy, not the use of military force. As a result, the death of Stresemann in 1929 was an important turning point for European relations, because his balanced approach to German foreign policy died with him.

The impact of the Great Depression

At the time of Stresemann's death, the system of European security established by Locarno remained intact. Germany still had no large army, navy or air force, the Rhineland was demilitarised and the authority of the League of Nations had not been challenged.

The event which enormously damaged European stability was the Wall Street stock market crash of October 1929 in the USA, which set in motion the greatest world economic crisis of the twentieth century. The world economy had become dependent for its stability, after the trauma of the First World War, on the prosperity of the US economy, especially the US banking sector, which had provided loans to European business. After the Wall Street collapse, US loans to Europe ceased. The result was widespread economic misery. In Britain, there was a financial crisis in 1931, which led to the formation of a 'National' government led by Ramsay MacDonald, the former Labour Party leader. The British government also introduced protective tariffs on foreign goods, thus abandoning its seemingly passionate adherence to free trade. Elsewhere in Europe, agricultural prices fell, trade collapsed, unemployment increased and many banks failed, most notably the Credit-Anstalt bank in Austria.

In the Asian Pacific region there were also severe economic problems. In Japan, unemployment rose, farm prices crashed and exports shrank. During 1930, a political crisis gripped Japan, leading inexorably to the collapse of democracy. In September 1931, the Japanese army occupied Manchuria (a province of China), triggering a major test of the credibility of the League of Nations. The Chinese government asked League members to invoke collective action against Japan's military aggression. A League of Nations commission, headed by the British peer Lord Lytton, was dispatched to Manchuria in order to resolve the dispute. The Lytton commission rebuked the Japanese government, but concluded that as Japanese claims to the region were convincing there was no need for military action or economic sanctions. Accordingly, Japan stayed in Manchuria but soon left the League of Nations. The Manchurian crisis was the first major test of the peacekeeping abilities of the League of Nations, which were shown to be somewhat more ineffective in action than they had appeared in theory.

The most acute effects of the Great Depression were felt in Germany. Between 1924 and 1929, Germany had paid £5 billion in reparations to the western Allies, but had received £9 billion in loans from the USA in return. Once these loans ended, in the months following the US stock market crash, the German economy descended into a deeply damaging depression. The number of unemployed, which stood at 1.4 million in 1928, soared to 6 million by 1932.

The political fall-out of the Great Depression in Germany proved equally devastating. Democratic government, always a fragile organism, very quickly collapsed. Article 48 of the Weimar constitution allowed the president to suspend parliament and rule under an 'emergency decree'. From 1930 to 1933, Germany was ruled by the whim of the nationalistic and undemocratic president, Paul von Hindenburg, a popular First World War army hero, who appointed several unpopular right-wing coalitions at a time when there was a quite remarkable surge of support for the extreme right-wing Nazi Party led by Adolf Hitler. This party had grown from relative obscurity in 1928 to become the largest political party in Germany by 1932. On 30 January 1933, Adolf Hitler was appointed German chancellor, after Hindenburg had exhausted his supply of other right-wing contenders.

It is very important to recognise the depth of the problems and the strains which the Great Depression placed on democratic governments in the 1930s. The widespread optimism of the Locarno period gave way to the self-preservation of the 'hungry Thirties'. Most countries abandoned free trade and turned away from schemes of international co-operation in trade and disarmament and towards trying to solve internal social and economic problems. Suddenly, totalitarian regimes, led by dynamic leaders, most notably Hitler, Joseph Stalin in the Soviet Union and Benito Mussolini in Italy, appeared to offer a way out of the misery of economic depression. The era of peaceful co-operation, ignited by Locarno in the 1920s, had been extinguished by the flood tide of depression even before Hitler came to power.

German foreign policy, 1929–33

It is often argued that Germany's dynamic and aggressive foreign policy which unfolded during the 1930s was the exclusive work of Adolf Hitler. However, such a view ignores the sharp change which took place in German foreign policy after the death of Stresemann and during the era of the Great Depression. As we have already seen, Stresemann's foreign policy worked in a peaceful and constructive manner to circumvent German obligations under the Treaty of Versailles. After Stresemann's death, there was a change in the tone and conduct of German foreign policy, which became much more openly aggressive, less co-operative with the other major European powers and more openly self-interested and unpredictable.

In March 1931, for example, the German government proposed a customs union between Germany and Austria, which was blocked only by very strong Allied pressure. That same year, the German government called for the return of Danzig from Poland (which was rejected) and also announced it would no longer be able to pay the reduced reparations payments outlined in the Young Plan (1929), which had reduced payments even further than the earlier Dawes Plan had done. At the Lausanne conference (1932) the Allies agreed to suspend

German reparations payments (which were never resumed). An even more ominous sign of the shape of things to come came in July 1932, when chancellor Franz von Papen gave the go-ahead to an accelerated programme of secret German rearmament. At the first meeting of the World Disarmament Conference in 1932, the German delegation walked out, refusing to return unless they were allowed to develop armed forces of a similar size to those of all the other major European powers. All of these provocative actions, which took place before Hitler came to power, show that German foreign policy was already moving in the direction of rapid rearmament to regain former military strength, and was already set firmly on a course to revise the Treaty of Versailles by unilateral action.

Document case study

Anglo-German relations, 1918–33

1.1 Reparations against Germany: the view of Winston Churchill

The economic clauses of the treaty [of Versailles] were malignant and silly to an extent that made them obviously futile. Germany was condemned to pay reparations on a fabulous scale. These dictates gave expression to the anger of the victors, and to the failure of their peoples to understand that no defeated nation or community can ever pay tribute [compensation] on a scale which would meet the cost of a modern war . . . No one in great authority had the wit, ascendancy, or detachment from public folly to declare these fundamental, brutal facts to the electorate; nor would anyone have been believed if he had. The triumphant allies continued to assert that they would squeeze Germany 'till the pips squeaked'. All this had a potent bearing on the prosperity of the world and the mood of the German race.

Source: W. Churchill, *The gathering storm*, London, 1948, pp. 22–24

1.2 The territorial losses of Germany under the Treaty of Versailles: the view of Lloyd George

You may strip Germany of her colonies, reduce her armaments to a mere police force and her navy to that of a fifth rate power, all the same, in the end, if she feels she has been unjustly treated in the peace of 1919, she will find means of exacting retribution of her conquerors . . . I cannot imagine any greater cause of future war than that the German people, who have proved themselves one of the most powerful and vigorous races in the world, should be surrounded by a number of small states, many of them consisting of peoples who have never previously set up a stable government for themselves, but each of them containing large masses of Germans clamouring for reunion with their native land.

Source: M. Gilbert, *The roots of appeasement*, London, 1966, pp. 189–90

1.3 The Treaty of Versailles: the view of Hitler, 1925

When in the year 1919 the German people was burdened with the peace treaty, we should have been justified in hoping that precisely through this instrument of boundless repression the cry for German freedom would have been immensely promoted. Peace treaties whose demands are a scourge to nations not seldom strike the first roll of drums for the uprising to come . . . We need to form a front against this treaty and engrave ourselves forever in the minds of men as an enemy of this treaty, so that later, when the harsh reality of this treacherous frippery would be revealed in its naked hate, the recollection of our attitude at that time would win us confidence.

Source: I. Lederer (ed.), *The Versailles settlement: Was it foredoomed to failure? The truth about the treaty*, London, 1960, pp. 86–90

1.4 The 'German problem' in the 1920s: a British view

I have to keep my eyes fixed on a date like 1960 or 1970, when Germany will be in a position, through one cause or another, to attack again if she wants to, and by that time there must have grown up in Germany a new generation who, whatever their feelings of resentment about the Treaty of Versailles, of the pain at the situation which the Treaty brought upon Germany, will yet say, after all, things must have an end . . . But if you are to have any chance of getting that kind of generation in Germany in 1960 or 1970 you must begin the work of pacification tomorrow.

Source: Sir Austen Chamberlain, evidence to the Committee of Imperial Defence, 1926, Public Record Office (CAB 2), London

1.5 The new world order after the Paris peace settlement: the view of the British Foreign Office, 1926

We have got all we want – perhaps more. Our sole object is to keep what we want and live in peace . . . The fact is that war and rumours of war, quarrels and friction, in any corner of the world, spell loss and harm to British commercial and financial interests . . . whatever else may be the outcome of a disturbance of the peace, we shall be the losers.

Source: *Documents on British foreign policy, 1919–1939, Vol. 1*, London, 1946, p. 846

1.6 Hitler on war, 1928

The task which therefore falls to all really great legislators and statesmen is not so much to prepare for war in a narrow sense, but rather to educate and train thoroughly a people so that to all intents and purposes its future appears inherently assured. In this way even wars lose their character as isolated, more or less violent surprises, instead becoming part of a natural, indeed self-evident pattern of thorough, well secured, sustained national development.

Source: G. Weinberg (ed.), *Hitler Zweites Buch. Ein Dokument aus dem Jahr 1928*, Stuttgart, 1978, p. 78

1.7 The British attitude to the Treaty of Versailles: the view of Ramsay MacDonald, the British prime minister, 1932

I do not believe that any of us can rigidly resist the German claim that the treaty of Versailles must in some respects be reconsidered. Supposing you were to continue to repeat 'No' to those claims, and Germany said 'Then as we are not to be released by agreement we shall appeal to the sense of fair play of the whole world and release ourselves reasonably'.

Source: *Documents diplomatiques français, 1932–1939, Vol. 1*, Paris, 1964, document no. 235

Document case-study questions

1 What is Churchill's view of the economic clauses of the Treaty of Versailles as outlined in 1.1?

2 According to Lloyd George in 1.2, how was the Treaty of Versailles flawed?

3 Explain what 1.3 tells us about the use that would be made of the Treaty of Versailles in Nazi propaganda.

4 Outline the British view, according to 1.4, of the likelihood of a German military revival in the mid-1920s.

5 What type of policy is the Foreign Office official advocating in 1.5?

6 Briefly discuss Hitler's attitude to war in 1.6.

7 What does 1.7 tell us about MacDonald's view of German grievances over Versailles?

2 The impact of Adolf Hitler: foreign-policy aims and actions, 1933–37

Adolf Hitler was appointed German chancellor on 30 January 1933. From 1933 to 1937, he consolidated his hold on power in Germany, built up armaments and pursued an extremely bold and dynamic foreign policy which escalated European tension step by step, eventually leading to the outbreak of the Second World War.

What were Hitler's aims in foreign policy?

Hitler's objectives in foreign affairs have been subject to microscopic scrutiny. The new dimensions of Hitler's foreign policy were his abandonment of the pre-1914 German desire for a world-wide colonial empire and the creation of a large navy. Even more distinctive was his burning passion about racial purity, which implied the destruction of the Jewish race. Hitler was deeply interested in Germany's position in the European system. In *Mein Kampf* ('My Struggle'), part autobiography, part political rant, published in 1925, Hitler outlined his key foreign-policy aims. The first aim, shared by most Germans, was to overturn the hated Treaty of Versailles. To achieve this objective, the German armed forces had to be rebuilt. However, the restoration of Germany as the major military power in Europe was merely the prelude to a very ambitious programme of territorial expansion, which went way beyond the restoration of the German borders of 1914. Hitler aimed, in the first instance, to incorporate all German-speakers in Austria, Czechoslovakia and Poland into an enlarged German Reich. The second – and dominant – aim of Hitler's foreign policy was to gain for Germany a vast quantity of 'living space' (*Lebensraum*) in eastern Europe. To reach this objective, Hitler intended, when he judged the time was ripe, to invade the Soviet Union, which would then be depopulated in the most ruthless manner, and to relocate Germans onto that territory.

Hitler appreciated that such a bold and adventurous programme of military aggression would be opposed by France (as well, of course, as the Soviet Union). Indeed, a war against France and Russia was always implicit in Hitler's long-term foreign-policy thinking. In order to improve Germany's diplomatic position in relation to these two major powers, Hitler hoped to persuade Britain, through skilful diplomatic efforts, to abandon its traditional support for a balance of power in Europe and to remain neutral in a future German bid for the mastery of the Continent. If Britain could not be persuaded to stand aside while Germany dominated Europe by force, then Hitler realised he might have to fight a combination of Russia, France and Britain, but he desperately hoped to avoid this situation. In order to disguise his ultimate objectives, Hitler intended to move slowly, stage by stage, in the achievement of his foreign-policy aims, concentrating exclusively on one objective at a time in order to confuse the other major European powers about his ultimate goal. He was also determined to give the false impression that this ultimate goal was only to overturn the Treaty of Versailles, in the hope of gaining British sympathy with this apparently limited objective.

The great difficulty among historians is to decide whether Hitler's aims, as outlined in *Mein Kampf*, were really a clear blueprint for foreign-policy action or a pipe dream. Any set of plans in the arena of international relations is always limited by military and economic resources. In the case of Germany, which did have the potential to be a dominant military power, these aims were not completely unrealistic, if Hitler could gain power. Once in power, Hitler did carry out most of his previously outlined aims in the manner he had envisaged. Even when he compromised or modified his aims, for example by signing the Nazi–Soviet pact in 1939 (see Chapter 5), it was done as a tactical ploy, in that instance in order to isolate Poland, and it did not lead Hitler to abandon his long-cherished objective of attacking the Soviet Union.

Given the strong support which already existed in Germany for overturning the Treaty of Versailles, and Hitler's own foreign-policy objectives, it was clear that from 1933 onwards Europe was on course, at the very least, for a very turbulent period.

The early years of Hitler's foreign policy, 1933–35

In the early years of Hitler's rule, Germany was still in a very weak military and economic position. Until the German armed forces were fully rebuilt, Hitler realised he would have to proceed with extreme caution in foreign affairs. It is hardly surprising, therefore, that his first speeches on foreign policy in 1933 stressed a desire for 'peace' and 'equal treatment' for Germany in European affairs. Indeed, Hitler's public speeches on foreign policy between 1933 and 1935 were more friendly and less belligerent than those of his immediate predecessors. The British government, very anxious to maintain good relations with Germany, offered a generally favourable response to these speeches. To most European diplomats Hitler's foreign policy appeared to represent continuity rather than a radical and aggressive new approach to European affairs.

Hitler's new approach to the Soviet Union

Yet there were some very important changes in German foreign policy enacted by Hitler shortly after he became chancellor. One of the most significant was a distinct cooling of relations with the Soviet Union. Germany and the Soviet Union had been on fairly good terms with one another ever since the signing of the Treaty of Rapallo in 1922. During the latter years of the Weimar era, the Soviet Red Army had allowed German troops and airmen to engage in secret training exercises on Soviet soil. On coming to power, however, Hitler adopted a much less friendly approach to the Soviet Union: his speeches struck a decidedly anti-communist and anti-Russian tone.

The deeply antagonistic stance which characterised German relations with the Soviet Union from 1933 onwards fitted in perfectly with Hitler's ultimate objective of gaining *Lebensraum* in eastern Europe at the expense of the Soviet Union, but it was not without its opponents within Germany. In September 1933, for example, the German foreign ministry actually questioned the wisdom of Germany adopting an anti-Russian stance and even suggested it was in the best interests of Germany to maintain cordial relations with Stalin's regime. Hitler responded to this advice by informing these officials that a restoration of good relations between Germany and the Soviet Union was 'impossible' under the Nazi regime.

Hitler's desire for good relations with Britain

A second noticeable change in German foreign policy under Hitler was his strong desire, especially in the early years of his rule, to improve Anglo-German relations. Indeed, he dreamed of an Anglo-German alliance in which Germany guaranteed the British empire in return for Britain allowing Germany a 'free hand' to dominate eastern Europe. Hitler was of the firm opinion that the pre-1914 Anglo-German antagonism, which had been characterised by strong naval rivalry, had been the chief reason why Britain had joined forces with France and Russia, a move which had denied Germany victory in the First World War. He believed that he must avoid a situation arising whereby Germany faced a combination of France, Britain and Russia. As a result, he looked for any opportunity to improve relations with Britain.

Germany withdraws from the League of Nations

The first major intervention into foreign affairs by Hitler was his decision in October 1933 to withdraw Germany simultaneously from the League of Nations and the much-hyped World Disarmament Conference. These decisions were very strongly supported inside Nazi Germany. Withdrawal from the League of Nations allowed Germany to act as a free agent in European affairs, while leaving the Disarmament Conference gave the German army the opportunity to push ahead with rearmament.

Hitler claimed that Germany was being refused equal treatment by the League of Nations and was also being prevented from rearming by the intransigence of the French government, which, he claimed, desired to keep the German armed forces in a permanent state of inferiority. Ramsay MacDonald, the British prime minister, interpreted Hitler's desire to rearm in a spirit of trust and under-standing, and viewed the French obsession with security as the main obstacle to a disarmament agreement. It was, of course, very difficult for the French government to accept that a German regime, led by such an extreme German nationalist as Hitler, should be granted the right to expand its armed forces with complete freedom.

Germany's relations with Poland

Hitler's tactical flexibility in foreign policy did make it difficult for diplomatic experts to predict whether he wanted peace or war. Hitler's policy towards the Polish government in the early years of his rule reveals the difficulties foreign diplomats faced in accurately assessing the Nazi leader's true aims. During the Weimar era, Germany's relations with Poland had been characterised by bitterness and antagonism. Ever since 1919, the German foreign ministry had adopted a very strong anti-Polish line, primarily because Poland had gained Upper Silesia, economic control over Danzig and a strip of land cutting off East Prussia from the rest of Germany (known as the 'Polish Corridor') under the terms of the Treaty of Versailles. Many of Hitler's speeches (before he came to power) had also struck a decidedly anti-Polish tone.

When Hitler became chancellor, the German foreign ministry advised him that no understanding with Poland was possible until the territorial disputes resulting from the Treaty of Versailles were settled. He decided to ignore this advice, because he realised there was great propaganda value in improving relations with Poland, a country which was generally regarded as the arch-enemy of German interests in eastern Europe. In January 1934, therefore, Hitler, in a quite surprising move, agreed to Germany signing a non-aggression pact with Poland, in spite of vociferous opposition from the German foreign ministry and Nazi activists, who believed he was abandoning Germany's territorial claims over the Polish Corridor and Danzig. In fact, Hitler's pact with Poland was an act of supreme duplicity, designed to give the very misleading impression that Germany had peaceful intentions in eastern Europe, when in actual fact an independent Poland had no part of Hitler's long-term plans. The only future for Poland, as far as Hitler was concerned, was for it to become a satellite power of Nazi Germany: a base camp for the eventual German attack on the Soviet Union and an area for expanding German *Lebensraum*. In the short term, however, the pact with Poland was a diplomatic success. It eased fears of possible German aggression in eastern Europe and weakened the influence of the French government over Poland. For its part, the Polish government was willing to be the recipient of German goodwill, but refused to become a Nazi satellite, preferring instead to keep on good terms with Germany, France and Britain. Indeed, when Hitler politely asked the Polish government to sign a military alliance in 1935, which was aimed against the Soviet Union, the Polish government refused to become involved in such a binding agreement with the Nazi regime.

Hitler's policy towards Austria

Hitler's very carefully manufactured image as a peacemaker suffered a jolt during the summer of 1934 because of events in Austria. Hitler had been born in Austria and had spent most of his early life there. It was the Nazi leader's passionate desire to bring about a union between Austria and Germany (known as the *Anschluss*). Indeed, most European diplomats expected Hitler to press a claim for the *Anschluss* at some point in the foreseeable future. However, Engelbert Dollfuss, the Austrian chancellor, was opposed to the idea. In June

1934, he banned the Austrian Nazi Party, which was already engaging, with Hitler's approval, in subversive activities designed to undermine Austrian independence. The following month, a group of Austrian Nazis broke into the office of the Austrian chancellor and killed him on the spot. The assassination of Dollfuss did not lead to the seizure of power in Austria by the Nazis, but it did provoke suspicions throughout Europe that Hitler had ordered the killing as a pretext for occupying Austria.

Whatever the truth or otherwise of these allegations, the murder of Dollfuss produced widespread condemnation among the Allies. Mussolini, the Italian Fascist dictator, sent four army divisions to the Austrian border in a firm gesture of support for the independence of Austria. The British and French governments made public statements which indicated they would oppose any Nazi takeover in Austria. In the face of this international pressure, Hitler was forced publicly to disclaim any German involvement in the murder of Dollfuss and to deny that he was preparing to occupy Austria. The whole episode revealed that Germany was not yet strong enough to adopt a bolder position over Austria. Indeed, the incident served to weaken Germany's diplomatic position because it encouraged much closer relations between Italy and France. In January 1935, for example, a Franco-Italian agreement was signed.

The problem of German rearmament

The diplomatic weakness of Germany, as revealed by the events surrounding the murder of Dollfuss, prompted Hitler to push ahead with German rearmament. In January 1935, he enjoyed a stunning diplomatic victory when the German-speaking population of the Saar coalmining region was allowed the choice in a referendum either to remain under League of Nations democratic rule or to be ruled by Hitler's Nazi regime. By an overwhelming majority, the inhabitants of the Saar opted to be ruled by the Nazi dictator.

In March 1935, Hitler took his first major gamble in European relations when he publicly announced that the German army (limited to 100,000 by the Treaty of Versailles) had already expanded to 240,000 and, through the introduction of conscription (prohibited by the treaty), would grow to 550,000 in less than three years. At the same time, Hitler made public the existence of a German air force (supposedly illegal under the terms of Versailles) and also announced plans for the rapid expansion of the German navy. All of this was common knowledge in the secretive world in which British, French and Italian diplomats moved, but the German announcement came as a great shock to the general public.

The Stresa Front

In response to public fears of the implications of German rearmament for European stability, leading representatives of the British, French and Italian governments met at Stresa between 11 and 14 April 1935 and issued a sternly worded joint declaration (dubbed the 'Stresa Front'), denouncing the 'unilateral repudiation' of the armaments limitation clauses of Versailles by Germany and pledging to act together to ensure there were no further breaches of international treaties by the Nazi regime. The Stresa Front was not an alliance aimed against Nazi Germany, nor did it propose any specific action which would be taken immediately or in the future to halt German unilateral breaches of international treaties. Nevertheless, Hitler was concerned enough by this apparent show of unity by the Allies to say in a keynote speech in May 1935 that Germany 'wants peace and desires peace'. He also held out the prospect of Germany taking part in future agreements to limit armaments. *The Times* claimed that Hitler's speech showed his 'sincerity and peaceful intentions'.

The French reaction to German rearmament

The French government reacted swiftly to the news of German rearmament by signing a treaty of mutual assistance on 2 May 1935 with the Soviet Union. This agreement was supplemented on 16 May 1936 by a diplomatic agreement between the Soviet, French and Czechoslovak governments. Under the terms of this arrangement, the French and Soviet governments agreed to come to the defence of Czechoslovakia in the event of an unprovoked attack by an outside power. Yet this treaty contained an ingenious get-out clause: France had to be actively defending Czechoslovakia from attack before the Soviet Red Army was obliged to become involved.

The Anglo-German naval agreement

The British government, peeved about the French decision to conclude two new agreements with the Soviet Union, outside of the auspices of the League of Nations, decided to adopt a conciliatory attitude to the German desire to rearm. In June 1935, the British government opened up naval disarmament negotiations with Germany. These discussions led quickly to the signing of the Anglo-German naval agreement, which limited new German naval vessels to 35 per cent of the existing strength of the Royal Navy. The Anglo-German naval agreement was of little hardship to Germany because it would take the German navy several years to reach the set limit. In essence, the naval agreement recognised Germany's right to rearm, and thereby endorsed Hitler's drive to breach the arms limitation clauses of the Treaty of Versailles. Even worse, the agreement severely undermined the unity of the Stresa Front. The whole episode proved to be a great diplomatic triumph for Hitler, who had greatly improved Anglo-German relations and driven a wedge between the Allies at one and the same time. The naval agreement was greeted with some enthusiasm in Britain, especially by those people who could remember that it was Anglo-German naval rivalry which had been one of the chief causes of antagonism between the two nations before the outbreak of the First World War.

The Italian invasion of Abyssinia and its consequences

In October 1935, the already fragile diplomatic unity between Britain, France and Italy fell apart when Italian troops invaded Abyssinia (modern-day Ethiopia).

The attack was not completely unexpected: successive Italian governments desired territorial expansion in Africa. There was also a widely held desire among Italian nationalists to avenge the humiliating Italian military defeat by Abyssinian troops at Adowa in 1896.

Even so, the Italian assault on Abyssinia came at a particularly bad time for Stanley Baldwin, the British prime minister, whose National government was fighting the 1935 general election under the slogan 'peace by collective security'. The British government was now faced with matching strong words with action. Sir Samuel Hoare, the British foreign secretary, hastily supported the imposition of economic sanctions by the League of Nations against Italy. The aim of the sanctions was to deny Italian forces war supplies, but oil was not included in the sanctions and many of the major oil suppliers – in particular the USA – were not even members of the League of Nations. In addition, the League of Nations took no military measures to enforce economic sanctions.

The Hoare–Laval pact

To make matters worse, the French government only half-heartedly supported the sanctions policy and was actually quite willing to accept Mussolini's invasion in case the Italian dictator became alienated from Britain and France and decided to move closer to Nazi Germany. For its part, the British government, which had been sprung into taking strong action against Italy, largely under the pressure of public opinion, was also having second thoughts about economic sanctions. Accordingly, Pierre Laval, the French foreign minister, met Hoare in Paris in December 1935 with the quite cynical objective of finding some way to allow Mussolini to keep hold of most of the territory already occupied by Italian troops in Abyssinia. After a brief discussion, Hoare and Laval agreed that Italian forces should retain most of Abyssinia, save for a very small strip of land along the coast (later dubbed by *The Times* as 'a corridor for camels'). However, the Hoare–Laval pact was leaked out to the press (by French diplomats), causing maximum political embarrassment for both the British and French foreign ministers. Hoare (who claimed he had acted without the agreement of the British government – which was a lie) was forced, by the sheer weight of public opinion, to resign as foreign secretary. He was replaced by Anthony Eden, at the age of 38 the youngest British foreign secretary since 1851, who had built up his own reputation on foreign affairs as a very firm supporter of the League of Nations. In France, the coalition led by Laval was also hounded out of office by public outrage.

What the Hoare–Laval pact had revealed was the very cynical attitude of both the British and French governments towards the principles of the League of Nations. In public, British and French ministers had expressed deep outrage against the Italian assault on Abyssinia, but in private they were quite willing to endorse Italian aggression. Without doubt, the Abyssinian crisis greatly damaged the already fragile credibility of the League of Nations. Even worse, Mussolini never really forgave the British and French governments for supporting economic sanctions against Italy. Indeed, in the aftermath of the Abyssinian affair, Mussolini drew Italy into a close diplomatic relationship with Nazi

Germany. Above all, the inept diplomacy of Hoare and Laval during the Abyssinian affair gave Hitler the clearest sign yet that Britain and France would not act to halt further acts of military aggression. The Abyssinian affair was, in so many ways, the green light for further acts of aggression.

The Rhineland crisis

In the early months of 1936, the British government discussed the likely impact of the Abyssinian affair on German foreign policy. Eden told the British cabinet in January 1936 that Hitler was likely to use the uncertainty created by the Abyssinian affair to begin the process of destroying the Treaty of Versailles. He suggested that Britain needed to increase its rearmament programme and to encourage Hitler to solve his foreign-policy grievances by peaceful negotiation rather than by taking unilateral action.

On 7 March 1936, however, Hitler did take such action, by ordering German troops to march into the demilitarised Rhineland. Hitler knew this was a gamble, as the German army was vastly inferior, at this time, to the French forces based in western Europe, and the deeply symbolic march of German troops over the Rhineland bridges clearly breached both the Treaty of Versailles and the Locarno treaties. The French government, without any assurance of British government support, offered a very strong verbal protest, but took no military action. The immediate reaction of the Belgian government to the Rhineland crisis was to announce that it would revert to a policy of neutrality in European affairs.

Hitler claimed his decision to send troops into the Rhineland had been prompted by the decision of the French government to ratify its treaty of mutual assistance with the Soviet Union on 27 February 1936. According to Hitler, this agreement had freed Germany from its obligations under the terms of the Locarno treaties.

The British public seemed to agree wholeheartedly with Anthony Eden's much-quoted Cockney taxi driver, who had told the foreign secretary while driving him to the House of Commons in his cab, that 'Hitler was only going into his own back garden'. By and large, the remilitarisation of the Rhineland was viewed by the British government as not only inevitable, but also justified. Indeed, British policy throughout the Rhineland affair can be termed 'passive appeasement', by which is meant that the settlement of a German foreign-policy grievance was accepted by the British government, albeit with some harsh words said about the method used by the Nazi regime to achieve its objective.

Hitler had solved the Rhineland problem by sudden unilateral action, without engaging in any negotiations with the Allies, just as Mussolini had done in Abyssinia. The decision by Hitler to act over the Rhineland in March 1936 sought to exploit the diplomatic chaos and ineptitude which had characterised British and French policy in the aftermath of the Abyssinian crisis. It seems that Hitler realised a German move into the Rhineland would not be met with more than censorious words of protest in Britain and France – and his judgement proved correct.

Overall, the Rhineland crisis revealed that the British government did not really object to Germany breaching the terms of the Treaty of Versailles, provided a legitimate German grievance was being expunged in the process. Of course, the British government would have liked Hitler to have pursued his policy over the Rhineland by negotiation. The Rhineland affair also showed Hitler that the French government would not use military force to uphold the Treaty of Versailles without a firm commitment of British military support.

The Spanish Civil War

The passive acceptance of the forward march of the European dictators by the British and French governments was further illustrated by the events surrounding the outbreak of a civil war in Spain. In February 1936, the Nationalists became the largest party grouping in the Cortes (the Spanish parliament), following national elections. But a Popular Front, composed of liberals, socialists and communists, formed a coalition to prevent the Nationalists taking power. General Francisco Franco, a leading commander of the Spanish army in Morocco, supported by a number of like-minded Nationalists and conservatives, refused to accept the rule of the Popular Front, preferring instead to establish an alternative government, thereby plunging Spain into a bitter civil war which lasted for three years.

The Spanish Civil War was viewed at the time as a major ideological struggle between communism and fascism. Germany and Italy offered considerable military aid to Franco's Nationalists, while the Soviet Union provided limited military support to the less well equipped Popular Front forces. The British and French governments agreed on a policy of non-intervention, which put paid to any chance of the Popular Front being able to defeat the Nationalists. Indeed, Franco's troops gained a comprehensive victory in 1939.

The turmoil in Spain further undermined the maintenance of peace through collective security. Spain also provided a very good training ground for the newly created German air force (the *Luftwaffe*). Indeed, the German bombing of Guernica sent shock waves through the civilian populations of Europe. In Britain and France, the policy of non-intervention widened political divisions between right and left over how to deal with the onward march of fascism in Europe. The British government claimed non-intervention was designed to prevent an escalation of the conflict. On the left of British politics, however, this view was not accepted and led to a hardening of attitudes against fascism, while on the Conservative right there was a corresponding movement after the outbreak of the Spanish Civil War towards the policy of appeasing the dictators.

Hitler moves from strength to strength

The outbreak of the Spanish Civil War also proved useful for Hitler in two ways: it diverted attention from the Rhineland crisis and the increasing build-up of German armaments. In September 1936, a Four Year Plan, designed to make

Germany self-sufficient in food and raw materials – and ready for war by 1940 – was introduced in a wave of publicity. Under the Four Year Plan, German imports were drastically reduced and financial and tax incentives were offered to those industries which produced synthetic products and to farmers who increased food production. The Four Year Plan was also accompanied by a rapid increase in spending on rearmament.

Overall, the year 1936 was unquestionably one of enormous success for Hitler in domestic and foreign policy. The Rhineland had been remilitarised peacefully. The German economy, greatly boosted by the rearmament programme and public spending programmes, was producing a dramatic fall in unemployment and a general 'feel good factor' throughout Germany. In July, an Austro-German agreement was signed in which the Austrian government agreed to accept German control of foreign policy in return for a vague promise to maintain the independence of Austria. In August, the Nazi regime was offered a great deal of praise – especially in the British, US and French media – for its 'efficient organisation' of the Berlin Olympic Games. In a quite startling act of appease-ment, the French Olympic team (but not the British) gave the Nazi salute in front of Hitler during the glittering opening ceremony.

In October 1936, Mussolini and Hitler signed the Rome–Berlin Axis, which brought the two fascist powers into even closer collaboration. Even more significantly, Mussolini dropped his former bitter opposition to the union between Germany and Austria. In November, Nazi Germany signed the much-heralded Anti-Comintern pact with Japan (later joined by Italy), which pledged its signatories to do all in their power to defeat 'the communist world conspiracy'.

By the end of 1936, therefore, Hitler's popularity in Nazi Germany stood at an all-time high, his diplomatic position was improving all the time and rearmament was restoring the German army to its pre-1914 position as the most powerful and feared in Europe.

The search for an Anglo-German alliance

There remained, however, one area of foreign policy in which Hitler had failed to make any significant progress: his long-cherished aim of concluding an Anglo-German alliance. In March 1936, therefore, Hitler appointed Joachim von Ribbentrop, a very committed and exceptionally loyal disciple, as German ambassador to Britain. Ribbentrop's chief objective was to secure an Anglo-German alliance, but his business background and rather opinionated and gauche manner did not go down well with the upper-class elite groups who ruled Britain in the 1930s. By the end of 1936, Ribbentrop had concluded that the British government was not very sympathetic towards Nazism and certainly not interested in signing an Anglo-German alliance which gave Germany a 'free hand' to dominate eastern Europe in return for a vague guarantee from Hitler not to invade Britain or interfere with the far-flung British empire. Indeed, the messages which Ribbentrop sent back to Berlin from London were increasingly anti-British in tone. They certainly encouraged Hitler to become – especially after 1936 – deeply pessimistic that he could gain an Anglo-German alliance on the terms he wanted.

It seems that Ribbentrop's anti-British views were deeply coloured by what he saw as his poor treatment in the company of the socially exclusive British upper classes. He was particularly outraged when his son was refused entry to Eton, at that time Britain's most exclusive public school. He was also alarmed about the anti-Nazi tone of several British newspapers. By May 1937, when Neville Chamberlain came to power, Ribbentrop had convinced Hitler that an alliance with the 'decadent' British government was impossible. Accordingly, he advised the Nazi dictator to base his future foreign policy on the prospect that the German desire for *Lebensraum* in eastern Europe was very likely to meet with resistance in western Europe by Britain and France.

Document case study
Hitler's foreign-policy aims and actions, 1933–37

2.1 Hitler's aims in foreign policy

We National Socialists [i.e. Nazis] must hold unflinchingly to our aim in foreign policy, namely, to secure for the German people the land and soil to which they are entitled on this earth . . . And I must sharply attack those folksy pen-pushers who claim to regard such an acquisition of soil as a 'breach of sacred human rights' and attack it as such in their scribblings . . . State boundaries are made by man and changed by man. The fact that a nation has succeeded in acquiring an undue amount of land constitutes no higher obligation that it should be recognised eternally . . . right lies in strength alone . . . Much as all of us today recognise the necessity of a reckoning with France, it would remain ineffectual in the long run if it represented the whole of our aim in foreign policy . . . But we must go further. The right to possess soil can become a duty if without extension of its soil a great nation seems doomed to destruction . . . Germany will either be a world power or there will be no Germany . . . And so we National Socialists consciously draw a line beneath the foreign policy tendency of the pre-War period. We take up where we broke off six hundred years ago. We stop the endless German movement to the south and west and turn our gaze towards the land in the east. At long last we break off the colonial and commercial policy of the pre-War period and shift to the soil policy of the future. If we speak of soil in Europe today, we can primarily have in mind Russia and her vassal border states.

Source: A. Hitler, *Mein Kampf*, London, 1969 edn, pp. 596–98

2.2 Hitler outlines his key objectives to the German generals, 1933

Building up of armed forces: Most important prerequisite for achieving the goal of regaining political power. National service [i.e. conscription] must be reintroduced. But beforehand the State leadership must ensure that the men subject to military service are not, even before their entry, poisoned by Pacifism, Marxism, Bolshevism or do not fall victim to this poison after their service. How should political power be used when it is gained? That is impossible to say yet. Perhaps fighting for new export possibilities, perhaps – and probably better – the conquest of new living space in the east and its ruthless Germanisation.

Source: J. Pridham and J. Noakes (eds), *Documents on Nazism 1919–1945*, London, 1974, pp. 508–09

2.3 The future course of German foreign policy: a British Foreign Office view, 1934

For the moment, Germany desires peace, for the reason that she is not prepared for war . . . Later she will presumably demand the territorial revision of the 'unjust' peace treaties . . . and will hope to secure these desiderata by peaceful means or at all events by the threat of force. If these methods fail, and the 'just' claims of Germany should lead to war, the blame will be laid on her enemies.

Source: *Documents on British foreign policy, Vol. 6*, London, 1957, pp. 975–90

2.4 Hitler's views on foreign policy, 1934

The struggle against Versailles is the means, but not the end of my policy. I am not in the least interested in the former frontiers of the Reich . . . we have to proceed step by step, so that no one will impede our advance. How I do this I don't yet know. But that it will be done is guaranteed by Britain's lack of firmness and France's internal disunity . . . I shall do everything in my power to prevent cooperation between Britain and France. If I succeed in bringing Italy and Britain to our side, the first part of our struggle for power will be greatly facilitated . . . We cannot, like Bismarck, limit ourselves to national aims. We must rule Europe or fall apart as a nation, fall back into the chaos of small states. Now can you understand why I cannot be limited, either in the east or in the west? . . . We alone can conquer the great continental space . . . We shall take this struggle upon us. It will open to us the door of permanent mastery of the world.

Source: H. Rauschning, *Hitler speaks: a series of conversations with Adolf Hitler on his real aims*, London, 1940, pp. 121–37

2.5 Hitler outlines the chief aims of the Four Year Plan, 1936

I hold it necessary that 100% self-sufficiency be introduced with iron decisiveness in all areas where this is possible . . . I would like to emphasise that I see in this task pure economic mobilisation with no cutting back in armaments firms . . . I therefore lay down the following task:

I The German army must be ready for combat in 4 years.

II The German economy must be capable of war in 4 years.

Source: J. Pridham and J. Noakes (eds), *Documents on Nazism 1919–1945*, London, 1974, pp. 401–10

2.6 The Hossbach memorandum, 1937

The aim of German policy was to secure and preserve the German racial community (*Volksmasse*) and to enlarge it. It was therefore a question of space . . . Germany had to reckon with two hate-inspired antagonists, Britain and France, to whom a German colossus in the centre of Europe was a thorn in the flesh, and both countries were opposed to any further strengthening of Germany's position either in Europe or overseas . . . Germany's problem could only be solved by force and this carried attendant risk . . . If the Führer was still living it was his unalterable resolve to solve Germany's problem of space at the latest by 1943–45.

Source: *Documents on German foreign policy, 1918–1945*, Series D, Vol. 1, London, 1949, pp. 29–30

2.7 Ribbentrop outlines Hitler's terms for an Anglo-German alliance, 1937

One day in 1937 I had a meeting with Herr von Ribbentrop, German Ambassador to Britain . . . We had a conversation lasting for more than two hours. Ribbentrop was most polite, and we ranged over the European scene, both in respect of armaments and policy. The gist of his statement to me was that Germany sought the friendship of England (on the continent we are still often called 'England'). He said he could have been Foreign Minister of Germany, but he had asked Hitler to let him come over to London in order to make the full case for an Anglo-German entente or even alliance. Germany would stand guard for the British Empire in all its greatness and extent. They might ask for the return of German colonies but this was evidently not cardinal. What was required was that Britain should give Germany a free hand in the East of Europe. She must have her *Lebensraum*, or living space, for her increasing population. Therefore Poland and the Danzig Corridor must be absorbed. White Russia and the Ukraine were indispensable to the future of the German Reich of some seventy million souls. Nothing less would suffice. All that was asked of the British Commonwealth and Empire was not to interfere. There was a large map on the wall and the Ambassador several times led me to it to illustrate his projects. After hearing this I said at once that I was sure the British government would not agree to give Germany a free hand in Eastern Europe . . . We were actually standing before the map when I said this. Ribbentrop turned abruptly away. He then said, 'In that case, war is inevitable. There is no way out. The Führer is resolved.'

Source: W. Churchill, *The gathering storm*, London, 1948, p. 203

Document case-study questions

1 Summarise the key aims of Hitler's foreign policy as outlined in 2.1.

2 What is Hitler's basic view about the future course of German policy in 2.2?

3 What does 2.3 tell us about Britain's view of how Hitler will act in foreign policy?

4 Offer an evaluation of any similarities or differences between the aims outlined by Hitler in 2.4 and those outlined in 2.1.

5 How useful is 2.5 for a historian assessing whether Hitler was cold-bloodedly making plans for war?

6 What implications are there for Britain and France in the views outlined in 2.6?

7 Using the evidence from 2.7, and evidence from the other sources above, offer an assessment of the likely course of German foreign policy under Hitler.

3 Why appeasement?

The policy which the British government adopted to cope with the dynamic foreign policy of Adolf Hitler in the 1930s was known as appeasement. The aim of appeasement was to satisfy German grievances through a process of negotiation. Explaining why this policy was chosen by the British government to deal with the revisionism of the European dictators in the 1930s is extremely difficult. Its adoption was not inevitable, nor was it the only one available.

The impact of the First World War

The First World War, viewed as the 'war to end all wars', had a profound impact on British society. The British public became disenchanted with the use of force to solve disputes among nations. War memorials listing the war dead were erected in every city, town and village throughout Britain. Anti-war poems, films and books were extremely popular with the general public. The annual day of remembrance (11 November), held to acknowledge the debt owed by Britain to those who had died in the First World War, was accompanied by a two-minute silence, which was religiously observed. There was also a very profound feeling, especially strong among the growing urban working class, that the 'land fit for heroes', promised by David Lloyd George, Britain's wartime leader, had failed to materialise. Indeed, by the 1930s it was generally felt that the First World War had been fought for no good purpose. This widespread public mood against war influenced the tone of political debate and the conduct of British foreign policy.

Faith in the League of Nations

There was an equally widespread faith among the British public in the League of Nations. A very large majority of British people saw the League as a better means of keeping peace in the world than military alliances backed by strong armed forces. The League of Nations Union, a major pressure group in British society, attracted over 400,000 members. Yet it was not fully appreciated by many of its most passionate supporters that the League of Nations could act as an effective peacekeeper in the world only as long as it retained the full backing of the great world powers. By 1937, only Britain, France and the Soviet Union, of the major powers in the world, were active members.

Sympathy with German grievances over the Treaty of Versailles

There was also a powerful feeling in British society that Germany had been punished much too harshly by the Treaty of Versailles. In 1919, John Maynard Keynes, the leading British economist, in a very influential book entitled *The economic consequences of the peace*, predicted the demand for £6.6 billion in reparations from Germany would cause economic chaos in Germany, destabilise world trade and lead to a widespread economic upheaval. When these prophecies came true, the view that the Treaty of Versailles had been unfair to Germany and required revision enjoyed very widespread popular support.

Economic difficulties

Britain suffered from a large number of economic and social problems during the inter-war period. The standard of housing, health care and education for the poorest members of society was very low. Unemployment rose in many of the previously prosperous industrial regions of the north of England and in many parts of Scotland, Wales and Northern Ireland. Most of the leading representatives of organised labour in the trade unions and the Labour Party believed that tackling pressing social problems such as high unemployment should be given a higher priority by the British government than building up costly armaments to deal with problems abroad. After the Wall Street crash of October 1929, Britain's economic problems grew worse, with unemployment soaring above the 3 million mark for the first time. In the aftermath of the Great Depression the National government (formed in 1931) became more concerned with Britain's internal economic problems and retaining its empire than with taking a deep interest in European problems.

The crisis of French will

France, Britain's major ally during the inter-war period, was also deeply troubled by political, social and economic problems. In French society there was also a very deep revulsion against war, but this was combined with a desperate longing for security from a possible future German attack. These French fears were not eased by the strong reluctance of the British government to offer the French government a firm military alliance. Without a definite pledge of British support to resist German aggression, French military chiefs adopted a purely defensive attitude and built a vast underground network of modern trenches along the western border with Germany (known as the Maginot line).

To make matters worse, French political life during the inter-war years was beset by corruption in high places, bitter differences between the left and the right, and a series of very unstable governments. There were three different coalition governments in power during 1932, four in 1933, two in 1934 and two in 1935. On the days when German troops entered the Rhineland (1936) and Austria (1938), France did not have a government. As the German threat grew more menacing, French foreign-policy makers, already impotent and defensive, tended to 'wait' for British support before deciding on any course of action or, rather, inaction. The leaders of France during the 1930s later claimed their own defensive position in response to the German threat to European peace was due to the British unwillingness to offer them a firm military commitment. However, there was very little support, or any real desire, on the part of the French government or army, or within French society more generally, to use force to halt German aggression.

Hostility towards Soviet communism

There was also great hostility in Britain (and France) to the communist Soviet Union. The news of Stalin's bloody purges among Soviet politicians, farmers and army officers increased this prevailing hostility. Indeed, communism, which aimed to destroy capitalist business, was viewed as a much greater threat among British business groups than fascism. To many Conservatives, and business groups, Hitler's Germany and Mussolini's Italy, dedicated to impeding the spread of communism, were objects of some admiration. As a result, there was strong opposition – especially in Britain – to an alliance with the Soviet Union aimed against the fascist powers.

The imperial dimension

Britain still maintained a vast world-wide empire during the inter-war years. As a result, British policy makers had to consider the views of self-governing colonies when considering foreign-policy action. Most of the self-governing dominions (Canada, Australia, South Africa and New Zealand) opposed giving military support to Britain in the event of a Second World War. The views of the growing nationalist movement in India also had to be taken into consideration. Under the 1935 Government of India Act, Indian nationalists had been promised self-government, and they were more concerned about achieving this than fighting for British interests in Europe. As the empire was such a vital market for British goods, these views could not be ignored. Indeed, there was a widely held view among British foreign-policy makers that if Britain engaged in another bloody European war the empire would collapse. This was something that could not be contemplated by the National government during the 1930s.

National defence

There is little doubt that the very impoverished state of Britain's military forces greatly influenced the adoption of the policy of appeasement. In 1935, for example, the British government commissioned a secret report on the condition and requirements of British national defence. This revealed that:

1 the Royal Navy was incapable of defending the empire and British trade;

2 the army was so small and so poorly equipped it could not offer much help to the French army in the event of a German assault;

3 the Royal Air Force had few bombers or fighter planes and totally inadequate air defence systems.

In these circumstances, the British government was urged by defence chiefs to increase spending on national defence, and to use diplomacy to prevent fighting a war against Germany, Italy and Japan simultaneously. The view of the defence chiefs had a profound influence on the leading figures in the National government – especially on Neville Chamberlain, the chancellor of the exchequer and future prime minister.

Navy

The key to British defence against overseas invasion was the Royal Navy. Britain had long been a leading maritime power. The same was true in the inter-war years. Britain maintained a naval fleet more powerful than any other in the world, with the exception of the USA, which had a navy of roughly equal strength. However, the vast world-wide imperial commitments the navy was expected to meet meant resources were dangerously overstretched. The fighting strength of the navy was also diminished by two important naval disarmament treaties, signed in Washington (1922) and London (1930), which left Britain with a somewhat out-of-date fleet. The naval chiefs advised the British government to ensure that British foreign policy was conducted so as to avoid a war breaking out against Germany, Italy and Japan; in the event of such a war the navy would need to maintain supremacy in the North Sea, the Mediterranean and the Pacific at the same time – which was something they felt would not be possible.

Army

The role of the British army (known as the 'Cinderella service') was always a secondary consideration in British defence policy. The British people had consistently opposed the imposition of conscription in peacetime. As a result, the British army was unique among the other leading European armies in that it was made up of volunteer soldiers. The 'voluntary principle' meant that few young people in Britain had any knowledge of military training and weaponry. Only during the latter stages of the First World War had Britain assembled a large army (including conscripts from 1916), but this was immediately reduced to its meagre pre-war levels once the war ended. In 1938, the British army numbered 387,000 troops, with over 75 per cent of this total engaged in defending the far-flung outposts of the British empire. Furthermore, this relatively small fighting force had equipment that was largely outdated; for example, very little attention had been given to the future use of tanks in a European war. In actual fact, spending on the army had the lowest priority in British national defence. In September 1938, at the very high point of the Munich crisis (see Chapter 4), Britain did not even have two fully equipped army divisions to send to France in the event of war breaking out.

For most of the inter-war period, British army chiefs had supported the doctrine of 'limited liability' for the British army in any future war. According to this doctrine, Britain would concentrate its efforts in a future European conflict on using naval and air power to support France rather than creating a vast conscript army. No leading general in the British army, nor any leading political figure, wanted a repeat of the horrific casualty rates suffered by British troops in the First World War. In essence, the British army had abandoned the idea of mounting another life-and-death struggle to halt Germany on land. The burden of fighting the German army in Europe was expected to fall disproportionately on the soldiers of the French army.

Air force

Of much more importance to British defence during the 1930s was the Royal Air Force (RAF). Air power was a new factor in defence thinking during the inter-war period. In 1921, Giulio Douhet, an Italian military expert, predicted that the use of aircraft in a future war would not only bring war home to the civilian population, but might provide a 'knock-out blow' which would decide the outcome of the war very quickly. The killing of civilians by the bombs of enemy aircraft was the new and terrifying prospect during the 1930s. As a result, spending on the air force rose to become the highest priority of national defence. Initially, British spending on the RAF concentrated on the building of bomber aircraft, designed to act as a deterrent, but in the late 1930s much more spending was devoted – especially after Neville Chamberlain became prime minister in 1937 – to building defence aircraft which could attack incoming bombers and thereby prevent large numbers of civilian casualties.

The Treasury view

The Treasury, the key government economic department, consistently opposed all-out British rearmament. In August 1919, the British government laid down the '10-year rule', which stipulated that spending on defence would be based on the prediction that there would be no major war for 10 years. The existence of this rule (which remained in force until 1932) led to a progressive reduction in defence spending. Even when spending on defence was increased (especially after February 1936), the Treasury stubbornly advised government ministers that vast spending on armaments in peacetime would severely impede the sluggish recovery of the British economy from the world depression. Rearmament would divert the already very limited supply of skilled British industrial workers into the armaments industry, and thereby damage the revival of important export and consumer industries. The Treasury also suggested that increased spending on armaments would increase inflation. In order to maintain a stable domestic economy, therefore, defence spending was subject to a very stringent list of priorities, with fighter aircraft at the top, followed by naval spending, but with the needs of the army being given the lowest priority of all and receiving, as a consequence, the smallest proportion of defence expenditure. Overall, the spending priorities set by the Treasury justified supporting the policy of appeasement.

The mass media

The British public was told about international events by the mass media, which was dominated during the inter-war period not by television, which was not widely available in Britain until the mid-1950s, but by the press, BBC radio and the cinema newsreels. Most people in Britain bought a daily and a Sunday newspaper, listened to the radio and went to the cinema at least once a week. *The Times*, the most influential British newspaper, was a strong supporter of the policy of appeasement. Other leading newspapers, most notably the *Daily Mail* and the *Daily Express*, also supported it. However, the *News Chronicle* and the *Daily Telegraph* were more critical of the idea of appeasing Hitler and Mussolini. BBC radio was also very supportive of the policy of appeasement. Indeed, radio coverage of foreign-policy issues was very severely restricted by government pressure. As a result, BBC radio hardly ever broadcast any criticism of the foreign policy of the British government. The cinema newsreels portrayed Neville Chamberlain at the time of the Czech crisis (see Chapter 4) as a noble politician on 'a mission of peace', and very rarely allowed any of the opponents of appeasement to give their side of the argument.

Public opinion

It is much more difficult to assess what ordinary members of the public thought of the policy of appeasement. Public opinion polls were in their infancy during the 1930s. Those which were taken show that the foreign policy most favoured by the British public was not the appeasement of the fascist dictators but the upholding of collective security through the League of Nations. In 1935, a nationwide opinion poll, known as the 'Peace Ballot', in which over 11 million people participated, revealed overwhelming support for collective security, but also showed equally overwhelming opposition to rearmament, which tends to indicate there was some confusion as to how a potential aggressor could be stopped. The idea of appeasing the European dictators directly was a more contentious policy. Indeed, once Hitler had occupied Czechoslovakia in March 1939, the vast majority of the British public supported the creation of a military alliance between Britain, France and the Soviet Union in order to halt German aggression in Europe.

The supporters of appeasement

The supporters of the policy of appeasement tended to come predominantly from what is known as the 'establishment', including most of the Conservative Party, upper-class aristocratic and business groups, several leading newspapers and the Church of England, but also from some right-wing extremist groups. The only significant group on the centre-left to offer support for appeasement was the pacifists, but they gave support because the policy favoured the upholding of peace. Most Conservatives wanted to avoid British military involvement in

European affairs and opposed closer relations with the Soviet Union. Many Conservatives, although not Nazis themselves, preferred Hitler's Nazi regime to that of the communist Soviet Union. These views were particularly strong among upper-class and aristocratic Conservatives, although they were shared by many in business and industrial circles.

Many committed supporters of appeasement visited Nazi Germany, as they believed that personal contact with the Nazi regime was the best means of encouraging cordial Anglo-German relations. They usually returned with glowing reports of the 'national awakening' which was taking place. The supporters of appeasement did not like to dwell on the 'nasty side' of life inside Nazi Germany, which they all knew about but chose to ignore. One very well known meeting place of upper-class and Conservative supporters of appeasement was Cliveden, the Buckinghamshire home of the Astor family, who owned the *Observer* newspaper. The 'Cliveden set' shared a number of attitudes, most notably a desire for a more active policy of appeasing the Nazi regime, a strong hostility towards the Soviet Union, a lack of faith in the French army and very little enthusiasm for the League of Nations.

The most high-profile supporter of appeasement within the upper class was King Edward VIII (who abdicated in 1936 in order to marry Mrs Wallis Simpson, an American divorcee). Edward strongly supported the policy of appeasement, even going so far as to visit Hitler after his abdication. It seems likely that, if Hitler had successfully invaded Britain during the Second World War, he would have offered Edward the opportunity to be his chosen Nazi leader, though it remains doubtful whether Edward would have accepted.

The Church of England (known by contemporaries as the 'Tory Party at prayer') shared the view that the Treaty of Versailles had been unjust to Germany and gave very enthusiastic endorsement to Chamberlain's drive for peace.

Fringe groups on the extreme right also gave support to appeasement. The most well known in this category was the British Union of Fascists (BUF), established by Sir Oswald Mosley. The BUF started life as a copycat and derivative variant of Mussolini's Fascist Party, but it later also copied many of the ideas of Hitler's Nazi Party. The BUF engaged in a number of violent demonstrations with its left-wing opponents but, unlike German National Socialism and Italian fascism, it had a strong anti-war outlook and argued that Britain should keep out of all problems in Europe. The BUF did give support to the policy of appeasement and, indeed, most of its supporters would have lived happily in a Nazi-dominated Europe which did not attempt to attack Britain or its empire.

A number of pacifist groups, most notably the Peace Pledge Union, also supported the policy of appeasement. These pacifists had no illusion about the brutal nature of Hitler's regime, but their hatred of war meant they were willing to endorse and accept many of Hitler's acts of aggression and they urged support for appeasement right up to the outbreak of war.

The logic of appeasement

We must not conclude that appeasement was inevitable or the only policy available. It is very important to realise that it grew out of a particular and unique set of circumstances. It was chosen by the British government from a number of alternative foreign policies (see below). There was, as we have seen, a definite and strong logic to appeasement. Britain was certainly not militarily prepared for war, and attempting to conciliate Nazi Germany in order to try to avoid a Second World War was not an unreasonable choice to make in the circumstances. When Neville Chamberlain became prime minister in 1937, he decided he would try to satisfy the German grievances left by the Treaty of Versailles, in the hope that this would encourage Hitler to live at peace with the rest of Europe. The policy of appeasement, therefore, recognised that Germany was in a very strong military position and attempted to solve German grievances by peaceful negotiation. In essence, its supporters believed appeasement was not only the most logical policy to follow, but also the only one which had any realistic chance of preventing war. It would be wrong, however, to believe that appeasement amounted to peace at any price. If Hitler intended to dominate Europe by force, then Chamberlain accepted, though with great reluctance, that force would have to be met by force.

Alternatives to appeasement

There were alternative policies available to deal with the German threat during the 1930s. One such policy was to support the upholding of collective security through the League of Nations. However, the League of Nations had failed to prevent the military aggression of Japan in Manchuria (1931) and Italy in Abyssinia (1935), and its credibility was severely undermined, primarily because Britain and France had not upheld its major principles during key moments of crisis. The machinery of the League did not work because those who operated it refused to use it effectively. In fact, Britain and France paid lip service to the ideals of the League, thereby turning a good idea into a discredited one. A collective response by all members of the League – even in 1939 – might have prevented war.

A second alternative policy to appeasement, championed most forcefully by Winston Churchill, was the idea of creating a grand military alliance of anti-fascist powers, led by Britain, France and the Soviet Union. Churchill argued that only the threat of military aggression stood any chance of deterring the European dictators. This policy, based on military strength, was certainly a realistic one. If it had been followed, it may have served to deter Hitler and might have stopped him earlier. A British–French–Soviet alliance would certainly have forced Germany to fight the Second World War on two fronts from the beginning. Unfortunately, the people who supported this policy were outside the positions of power in the British government.

Critics of appeasement

The critics of appeasement, although not a unified group, included a broad spectrum of British public opinion, most notably factions in the Foreign Office and the Conservative Party, clustered around Churchill and Anthony Eden, most of the members of the Labour and Liberal parties, supporters of the League of Nations, trade unionists and many left-wing groups and intellectuals. They mostly supported the idea of the upholding of collective security through the League of Nations. They believed that Chamberlain's idea of satisfying the grievances of these dictators, from a position of military weakness, was more likely to encourage further aggression than deter it. These critics took the view that Hitler was essentially unappeasable. They also highlighted a clear difference in principle between the appeasement of legitimate grievances, granted within a spirit of equality, and the appeasement of the desires of a war-mongering dictator such as Adolf Hitler.

The critics of appeasement, although not in control of the leading positions in government, did come increasingly to represent the views of the majority of British public opinion. A public opinion poll in February 1939, for example, revealed that only 28 per cent of the British public thought that appeasement would bring lasting peace. In July 1939, 85 per cent of the British public supported the creation of a grand alliance to stop Hitler, the very same alliance which Churchill and his supporters were calling for. Indeed, the tremendous unity against Nazi Germany in Britain during the Second World War was due much more to the work of the critics of appeasement than to those who had advocated support for the policy of appeasement.

Document case study
Why appeasement?

3.1 Public opinion: the Peace Ballot, 1935

Question 1: Should Britain remain a member of the League of Nations?
Yes   10,642,560 (97%)
No   337,964   (3%)

Question 2: Are you in favour of an all-out reduction of armaments by international agreements?
Yes   10,058,026 (92.5%)
No   815,365   (7.5%)

Question 5a: Do you consider that, if a nation insists on attacking another, the other nations should combine to stop it by economic and non-military measures?
Yes   9,627,606 (94.1%)
No   607,165 (5.9%)

Question 5b: Do you consider that, if a nation insists on attacking another, the other nations should combine to compel it to stop by, if necessary, military measures?

Yes   6,506,770 (74.2%)

No   2,262,261 (25.8%)

Source: A. Livingstone, *The Peace Ballot: the official history*, London, 1935, pp. 49–51

3.2 The press: the view of Geoffrey Dawson, editor of *The Times*, on appeasement

Personally I am and always have been anxious that we should 'explore every avenue' in search for a reasonable understanding with Germany . . . The more personal contact there is between the two nations the better . . . I do my utmost night after night to keep out of the paper anything that might hurt their [German] susceptibilities . . . I have always been convinced that the peace of the world depends more than anything on our [Britain] getting on better relations with Germany.

Source: J. Wrench, *Geoffrey Dawson and our Times*, London, 1955, p. 364

3.3 German aims in Europe: the view of a leading supporter of appeasement

German foreign policy today is derived from the new fundamental outlook created by the revolution [when Hitler came to power in 1933]. The rise of consciousness of German nationhood which is now being experienced must necessarily relate itself to questions in Austria and Czechoslovakia. The dynamic of national liberation will not exhaust itself until these two questions are resolved. The process is inevitable. The sense of nationhood in the German mind today carries with it the recognition of the 'divine right' of other peoples to existence and independence. The integrity of the countries of eastern Europe is equally in no danger from such a philosophy.

Source: Speech by Lord Mount Temple, quoted in *The Times*, 26 February 1938

3.4 A critical view of appeasement: Clement Attlee, the Labour leader, 1938

The Labour movement has warned the country since 1932 that yielding to aggression in one part of the world means an increase in aggression in another. We are now paying in anxiety for a wrong foreign policy assumed since Labour was thrown out of office [in 1931]. I pray to heaven that we will not have to pay in blood.

Source: *The Times*, 19 September 1938

3.5 A communist poet contrasts Soviet communism with fascism, 1938

The consistent and unwavering fight of the USSR [the Soviet Union] to preserve peace at almost any cost, its willingness to make concessions for peace and its complete freedom from any aggressive aims, is contrasting more and more sharply with the military antics of the Fascist powers and the shiftiness and two-faced policies of 'democratic' Britain and France. It is becoming patently clear that Soviet communism not only stands for peace but is winning all along the line on the economic front, whereas Fascism is heading for war and economic disaster.

Source: P. Sloan (ed.), *John Cornford – a memoir*, London, 1938, pp. 159–69

3.6 The relative armed strengths of the European powers, 1938–39

Army strength (expressed as fully equipped army divisions)

	January 1938	August 1939
Germany	81	130
Great Britain	2	4
France	63	86
Italy	73	73
Soviet Union	125	125
Czechoslovakia	34	None
Poland	40	40

Air force strength (represented as number of available aircraft)

	January 1938	August 1939
Germany	1,820	4,210
Great Britain	1,050	1,750
France	1,195	1,234
Italy	1,301	1,531
Soviet Union	3,050	3,361
Czechoslovakia	600	None
Poland	500	500

Naval power (August 1939)

	Battleships	Aircraft carriers	Submarines
Germany	5	None	65
Great Britain	15	6	57
France	7	1	78
Italy	4	None	104
Soviet Union	3	None	20

Source: A. Adamthwaite, *The making of the Second World War*, London, 1977, pp. 227, 228

3.7 National defence: the view of Chamberlain, 1937

It was true, as the Chiefs of Staff had pointed out, that we could not hope to confront Germany satisfactorily and, when we looked round as to what help we could get from other nations, the results were not very encouraging. France was our most important friend. Though she was strongly defensive and possessed a powerful army, the French air force was far from satisfactory . . . A long time may elapse before France could be able to give us much help in the air. The power that had the greatest strength was the United States of America, but he would be a rash man who based his calculations on help from that quarter. Our position in relation to the small powers was much better than formerly, but he [Chamberlain] did not think that they would add much to our offensive or defensive strength. In time of peace their support was useful, but in war less so. The Chiefs of Staff, as he had mentioned, said they could not foresee the time when our defence forces would be strong enough to safeguard our territory, trade and vital interests against Germany, Italy and Japan simultaneously. They had urged that our foreign policy must be governed by this consideration, and they had made rather a strong appeal to this effect . . . As he himself had pointed out before, Germany was the real key to the question. In the light of the recent consideration given by the Cabinet to the question of improving relations with Germany, it was necessary to develop that theme further.

Source: Cabinet papers, 8 December 1937, Public Record Office (CAB 29/90/A), London

Document case-study questions

1 Comment briefly on what 3.1 reveals about the views of the British public towards the League of Nations, disarmament and collective security.

2 What conclusion can be drawn about the attitude of *The Times* editor towards Germany from the evidence in 3.2?

3 Explain Mount Temple's basic view of the aims of Hitler's foreign policy, as outlined in 3.3?

4 What does Attlee imply in 3.4 is the major reason for the international tension?

5 Why might you have reservations about regarding 3.5 as a true reflection of Soviet foreign policy?

6 Using 3.6, outline the relative military strengths of Britain and Germany.

7 What does 3.7 tell us about Chamberlain's favoured course of action in foreign policy?

4 Chamberlain and appeasement (1): the period of hope, May 1937 – October 1938

Neville Chamberlain became British prime minister in May 1937. With single-minded determination, he transformed appeasement from the passive acceptance of unilateral breaches of the Paris peace settlement by Nazi Germany into an active and positive mission to discover what the grievances of the European dictators were, and to try to satisfy them by peaceful negotiation.

Neville Chamberlain: early life and character

Neville Chamberlain was born in Birmingham in 1869. He was the eldest son of the Conservative imperialist Joseph Chamberlain and the half-brother of Sir Austen Chamberlain, the British foreign secretary who had helped to negotiate the terms of the Locarno treaties. Neville Chamberlain's early career was spent in business. He was also a leading figure in Birmingham politics, rising to the position of lord mayor. He entered parliament in 1918, aged 49, as the Conservative MP for the Birmingham Ladywood constituency. It was a comparatively late start on the national stage of politics but, following the fall from power of Lloyd George in 1922, Chamberlain's political career advanced quickly to high office under the astute guidance of Stanley Baldwin, the Conservative leader from 1923 to 1937 (Lloyd George held a low opinion of Chamberlain's political ability, which was reinforced by his poor performance as postmaster general in his coalition government). As minister of health (1924–29), Chamberlain made a noteworthy impact in the area of health and housing reform. As chancellor of the exchequer (1931–37), he was largely responsible for putting the British economy on a more stable footing after the trauma of the Great Depression. When Baldwin stood down as prime minister in May 1937, Chamberlain was his natural and undisputed successor.

Chamberlain has been frequently depicted by historians (especially those writing in the immediate post-war era) as a weak, cowardly and indecisive politician. It is important to appreciate that this one-dimensional view is unreliable. It is more accurate to view him as a competent, strong-willed and clear-sighted politician who followed the policy of appeasement because he believed that it was the only one with any chance of preventing war in Europe.

Chamberlain's views on the European crisis

When Chamberlain came to office, the international situation was in a state of great uncertainty. Hitler appeared set, at the very least, on the path of unilateral treaty revision and, possibly, on an attempt to dominate Europe by military force. Mussolini, the Italian leader, remained a very unpredictable dictator with territorial ambitions of his own. The bitter Spanish Civil War raged on without an end in sight. In the Far East, China and Japan were on the brink of war. Indeed, the deepening tension of international relations dominated Chamberlain's tenure as prime minister.

Chamberlain believed that differences between nations should be solved by negotiation. He also felt that British foreign policy under Baldwin had drifted in a rudderless fashion during a period fraught with danger. He had little faith in the ability of the League of Nations to prevent war and he was opposed to the formation of military alliances which might divide Europe into rival ideological blocs. Of the two varieties of European dictatorship, Chamberlain preferred to deal with the fascist regimes rather than the communist and anti-capitalist Soviet Union. He ruled out building closer relations with the democratic USA because he thought that President Roosevelt and most of the American people were wedded to the policy of isolationism. In assessing the state of the world in 1937, and the policy options available, Chamberlain decided that the chief aim of British foreign policy would be to improve relations with the dictator states of Germany and Italy.

Chamberlain's new direction

The military strategy underpinning Chamberlain's conciliatory diplomacy was based purely on defence. It involved the Royal Navy mounting a blockade of Germany, with RAF fighters preventing German air superiority over the British Isles. Chamberlain felt it was the duty of the French army to shoulder the major responsibility of holding German forces in western Europe in the event of war. This defence strategy offered very little tangible support to the French army and ensured that Britain would face a battle for survival – most probably alone against Nazi Germany – if the French army was unable to resist German aggression. Indeed, Chamberlain's defensive outlook made a conciliatory form of diplomacy, designed to prevent war in Europe, the only logical choice in the circumstances.

One of Chamberlain's key supporters in his drive to appease Hitler was Sir Nevile Henderson, the British ambassador in Berlin from 1937 to 1939. Henderson, who was secretly dubbed by his critics within the Foreign Office 'our Nazi ambassador in Berlin', was a passionate and obstinate supporter of the policy of appeasement. He reported very little of the 'nasty' details of Nazi rule, but instead sent upbeat dispatches from Berlin which constantly stressed that Hitler's aims in Europe were limited to a revision of the Treaty of Versailles and that he did not want to dominate Europe by military force.

The Halifax visit

The first real opportunity to open up direct negotiation with the Nazi regime came in November 1937, when Lord Halifax, a close adviser to Chamberlain on foreign affairs and another keen supporter of the policy of appeasement, was invited to attend a hunting exhibition attended by leading Nazis. Chamberlain decided that Halifax should use the visit to open talks with Nazi leaders, with the aim of improving Anglo-German relations. Anthony Eden, the foreign secretary, was somewhat sceptical about the idea of opening new talks with Nazi Germany

YET ONE MORE CONVERSATION

" *The time had come,*" Herr HITLER *said,*
" *To talk of many things,*
Of might and right and swastikas
And triangles and rings,

And why the world is boiling hot,
And whether Peace has wings."
Lord HALIFAX. "But not about Colonies."
Herr HITLER. "Hush!"

This cartoon appeared shortly after the visit of Lord Halifax to Germany in November 1937. The cartoon suggests that Halifax merely listened to a long speech by Hitler rather than engaging in a constructive diplomatic discussion with him about the prospects of peace in Europe.

because he did not think they would lead anywhere. Similarly, many leading diplomats in the Foreign Office also doubted whether it was wise to discuss the future of Europe with Hitler from a position of military inferiority. Indeed, the Foreign Office felt it was better to speed up rearmament and 'keep Hitler guessing' about what Britain might do in the event of further breaches of the Treaty of Versailles. Chamberlain ignored this advice and urged Halifax to take up the invitation to visit Nazi Germany.

Halifax arrived in Berlin on 17 November 1937. During his short visit he met with three of the leading Nazis: Hitler, Göring and Goebbels. In his meeting with Hitler, Halifax told the Nazi leader that the British government was not opposed to the peaceful settlement of German grievances over Austria and Czechoslovakia. In reply, Hitler claimed all he wanted from the British government was a 'free hand' to settle problems in central and eastern Europe. Chamberlain described the Halifax visit (which had not achieved anything tangible) as 'a great success' because it had created a friendly atmosphere between Britain and Germany.

The Hossbach memorandum

Hitler attached very little importance to the Halifax visit. In fact, he viewed it as an unwelcome intrusion into his own plans and schemes. Even before Halifax arrived in Germany, Hitler had already decided he would fight a war against Britain and France if they opposed his foreign-policy aims. On 5 November 1937, Hitler met a very carefully chosen group of key military leaders to discuss the future course of German foreign policy. A record of the meeting was kept by Colonel Hossbach (and so is known as the 'Hossbach memorandum'). During the meeting, Hitler claimed the chief aim of German foreign policy was the conquest of living space in eastern Europe, which had to be achieved between 1943 and 1945, while Germany still enjoyed a significant military advantage over its potential enemies. As a preliminary step towards the achievement of this ultimate goal, Austria and Czechoslovakia would have to be seized, which Hitler thought would probably provoke a major war with Britain and France, described by Hitler as 'two hate-filled antagonists'. Hitler told his generals that he was fully prepared to run the risk of a war with France and Britain in order to gain substantial territory in eastern Europe at the expense of the Soviet Union.

A great deal of discussion among historians has taken place over the significance of the Hossbach meeting. Some view it as evidence of a firm Nazi plan for a war with Britain and France as a consequence of the German seizure of Austria and Czechoslovakia. Other historians disagree, preferring instead to view the Hossbach meeting as a mere 'pep talk' by the Nazi dictator to a group of sceptical army generals, most of whom were opposed to a war with France and Britain. In more recent times, historians have tended to view the Hossbach meeting as a very significant event, marking the beginning of a provocative era of German foreign policy from early 1938 onwards.

Hitler makes key changes

In the months following the Hossbach meeting, Hitler did undertake a very significant reshuffle within the Nazi government, which involved moderate conservatives in key posts being sacked and replaced by Nazi extremists. General Werner von Blomberg and Colonel-General Werner von Fritsch, two leading army 'moderates' who had actually expressed opposition to Hitler's expansionist aims in Europe at the Hossbach meeting, were forced out of office after a carefully orchestrated character assassination of them both in the German press. Hitler appointed General Wilhelm Keitel as chief of the armed forces and made himself the overall commander of the armed forces. During the same period, the pro-Nazi Ribbentrop replaced the moderate Neurath as foreign minister. These changes in the key posts controlling the foreign ministry and the army greatly strengthened Hitler's control over foreign policy and national defence, which in turn led to a more aggressive stance in foreign affairs by Hitler during 1938 and 1939. Hence, Chamberlain's passionate drive to appease Hitler took place at a time when the Nazi dictator was heading in the opposite direction.

Chamberlain's conflict with the Foreign Office

Chamberlain also made a significant change in the Foreign Office shortly after the Halifax visit. In December 1937, he decided to move Robert Vansittart, a well-known critic of Hitler and the Nazis and a sceptic over the policy of appeasement, from his very important foreign-policy role as permanent under-secretary at the Foreign Office to the virtually powerless role of chief diplomatic adviser to the government, a role in which he exerted no influence over foreign policy. Indeed, Chamberlain took more advice on foreign policy from Sir Horace Wilson, a fervent supporter of appeasement, with no diplomatic experience, who became his chief diplomatic envoy.

Chamberlain's increasing desire to push ahead with his policy of appeasing the dictators also led to a bitter conflict with Anthony Eden, the foreign secretary. In January 1938, Eden was quite horrified to learn on his return from a brief vacation on the French Riviera that Chamberlain had rejected out of hand (without consulting him) a proposal from Franklin D. Roosevelt, the US president, to convene an international conference of all the major powers, designed to establish agreed principles of international conduct. Eden fought bravely to keep Roosevelt's proposal on the table, but the US president, disappointed by Chamberlain's extremely lukewarm response to it, promptly dropped the idea in order to allow the British prime minister the opportunity to test his view that face-to-face negotiations with the dictators represented a better way of bringing about lasting peace in Europe.

In February 1938, Chamberlain decided to open up fresh talks with Mussolini with a view to improving Anglo-Italian relations. Eden was extremely hostile to this idea as he believed the unpredictable Mussolini could not be trusted. Yet

Chamberlain, with the full support of the cabinet, overruled Eden's views and gave the go-ahead to fresh talks with the Italian government. On 20 February 1938, Eden, believing his authority as foreign secretary was being completely undermined by Chamberlain, resigned, citing 'irreconcilable differences' with the prime minister over foreign policy as the chief reason for his departure. Eden was replaced by Halifax, the loyal supporter of the policy of appeasement who had earlier visited Nazi Germany.

The resignation of Eden

The dramatic resignation of Anthony Eden has been the subject of much discussion among historians. Some argue that a fundamental clash of personalities, not of policy, lay at the heart of Eden's decision to go. They point out that the 'temperamental' Eden resigned over British policy towards Italy, not over improving relations with Germany, a policy which it is claimed Eden had shown no real opposition towards in his entire time as foreign secretary. Other historians have suggested that there were fundamental differences over foreign policy between Chamberlain and Eden. They suggest that Eden did not believe that appeasement of the dictators, operating as a form of crisis management, could succeed with Hitler and Mussolini. It seems Eden wanted to extend the number of Britain's potential allies by improving relations with France and the USA, and by strengthening links with the Soviet Union, through the League of Nations, rather than making the appeasement of the dictators the single objective of British foreign policy. On the other hand, Chamberlain wanted to concentrate on appeasing the grievances of the most likely 'troublemakers' in Europe – Hitler and Mussolini – in the hope this would pave the way to long-term stability in Europe. It was this different outlook towards the international situation which put Chamberlain and Eden at loggerheads and led them to mistrust each other's motives and actions on foreign policy.

It is, indeed, pretty clear that Chamberlain, whether consciously aware of it or not, did often undermine Eden's authority as foreign secretary in such a way as to convince him he could no longer carry out his role. It seems that Chamberlain preferred a 'yes man' as foreign secretary, who carried out his policy, not a foreign secretary with too much of a mind of his own, especially one such as Eden who proved willing to cast doubt on his decisions and to propose alternative courses of action.

The union between Germany and Austria

Shortly after Eden resigned, Hitler made another dramatic intervention in foreign affairs by seizing control of Austria in March 1938. Hitler never made any secret of his desire to unite his native country with Germany when the time was right. In January 1938, Kurt von Schuschnigg, the Austrian leader, asked Hitler to call on Nazi activists to cease their disruptive activities in Austria. On 12 February 1938, Schuschnigg met with Hitler in order to discuss Nazi agitation in Austria. At the meeting, Hitler gave the Austrian leader no assurance whatsoever about restraining the Austrian Nazis. On the contrary, Hitler advised Schuschnigg to give key government posts to two leading Austrian Nazis, one of whom he wanted to be placed in charge of internal security.

On his return to Vienna, Schuschnigg, upset by the bullying way he had been treated by Hitler, decided to call a referendum, asking voters to support Austrian independence. This show of defiance by the Austrian leader outraged Hitler, who placed pressure on the Austrian government to call off the proposed referendum. On 11 March 1938, Göring, in a series of frantic telephone calls, persuaded Mussolini to support a Nazi takeover in Austria and then forced Schuschnigg to announce his resignation. He was replaced by Arthur Seyss-Inquart, a leading Austrian Nazi, whose first act as the new Austrian leader was to invite Hitler to occupy the country. On 12 March 1938, German troops, riding aboard heavily armoured tanks, drove into Austria, to be greeted by cheering crowds. A few hours later, Hitler crossed the Austrian border and received a rapturous reception from the people lining his route. He was so moved by the adulation shown to him by the Austrian people that he immediately decided to go ahead with the union between Austria and Germany. The achievement of the *Anschluss*, though completed by the bullying and intimidation of the Austrian government, was not a carefully planned invasion, but a supreme example of how Hitler often exploited the opportunities provided to him by unforeseen circumstances. Chamberlain issued a polite protest about the Nazi takeover in Austria, but he put most of the blame for the escalation of the crisis on Schuschnigg's 'rash' decision to call a referendum. The French government, in a state of disarray when the Nazis took over Austria, also accepted the *Anschluss* as an accomplished fact.

The Czech crisis

The focus of European attention now switched to the extremely vulnerable position of Czechoslovakia. From March to October 1938, the uncertain fate of 3.5 million German-speakers located in a border region of Czechoslovakia known as the Sudetenland brought Europe to the verge of war. Hitler claimed the Sudeten Germans were a persecuted minority who desired the right of self-determination. To back up this claim, Hitler gave substantial financial aid to the Sudeten German Party, a clone Czech Nazi Party, led by Konrad Henlein.

The idea of the Sudeten Germans being offered self-government directly threatened the independence of the Czechoslovak state, which was composed of a number of differing nationalities and had been created by the 1919 Paris peace conference. Czechoslovakia, led by Edvard Beneš, had developed into a model central European democracy, and was not an intolerant oppressor of minority groups (unlike the Nazi regime). Indeed, the Czechoslovak government was quite willing to offer greater local government to the Sudeten Germans, but was not prepared to grant them complete independence.

What made the Czech crisis so potentially dangerous for European peace was the existence of a number of inter-linked and complicated diplomatic agreements involving Czechoslovakia, France and the Soviet Union. One of these was a seemingly binding diplomatic agreement in which France and the Soviet Union were pledged to defend Czechoslovakia from an unprovoked attack by any foreign power. It was quickly realised that this agreement held out the real possibility of the Czech crisis resulting in the outbreak of a European war. However, the position of Czechoslovakia was more secure on paper than in reality. The two major powers – France and the Soviet Union – that had guaranteed Czechoslovak independence had put a subtle get-out clause into the agreement: France had to be actively defending Czechoslovakia from military attack before the Soviet Union was obliged to come to its defence. Neville Chamberlain was quite appalled at the prospect of France being drawn into a European war over Czechoslovakia and was determined to solve the Czech crisis by peaceful negotiation.

The May crisis

Throughout the spring of 1938, the tension between Germany and Czechoslovakia intensified. In May, a rumour circulating European capitals indicated that German troops were massing near the Czech border. This rumour (which was untrue) was spread by the Czechoslovak government in order to test the strength of support from its allies. The French and Soviet governments did pledge support to Czechoslovakia. However, Hitler was so outraged by the Czech government that he promptly summoned his leading generals on 30 May 1938 to a meeting at which he ordered them to immediately draw up a plan (known by the secret code name Case Green) to attack Czechoslovakia on 1 October 1938.

The Runciman mission

Chamberlain was so alarmed by the 'May crisis' that he became determined to find a peaceful solution to the Sudeten problem. In July 1938, he sent Lord Runciman, a Liberal shipping magnate, to Czechoslovakia as a mediator between the Czechoslovak government and the Sudeten German Party. During his discussions with both sides, Runciman, whom no one believed was really an independent mediator, least of all the Czechoslovak government, became extremely sympathetic towards the demand of the Sudeten Germans to be allowed the opportunity to join the Third Reich. The Czechoslovak government was willing to grant some form of self-government to them but not independence. As a result, the Runciman mission failed and he returned home empty-handed.

Chamberlain's dramatic visits to Hitler

The Czech crisis reached boiling point during September 1938. On 7 September, *The Times* published an editorial which suggested that the best way of solving the crisis would be for Czechoslovakia to allow the Sudetenland to be incorporated into the Third Reich. Although Halifax, the foreign secretary, denied that the views of *The Times* represented the thinking of the British government, most European leaders thought otherwise. On 12 September 1938, Hitler, speaking at the annual Nazi conference at Nuremberg, claimed the Sudeten Germans were 'not defenceless and not alone', giving a clear indication that he would soon take steps to solve the crisis by military force.

In the light of the very critical nature of the situation, Chamberlain decided to fly to Germany to meet with Hitler in a last-gasp attempt to find a negotiated solution. On 15 September 1938, Chamberlain met Hitler at Berchtesgaden, his retreat high up in the Bavarian hills. The chief objective of the visit was to discover what Hitler wanted and to try to give it to him. Hitler told Chamberlain that he wanted all districts of Czechoslovakia in which German-speakers were in the majority to be transferred to the Third Reich or he would settle the matter by force. Hitler never expected that Chamberlain could possibly get Czechoslovakia to accept these demands.

In the following week, however, Chamberlain persuaded the British cabinet, the French government and the Czechoslovak government – the last with much coercion – to accept Hitler's demands. In essence, Britain and France told the Czechoslovakians to accede to Hitler's demands or they would abandon them completely. The Soviet government, which was prepared to fulfil its obligations towards Czechoslovakia, was not even consulted in these negotiations. It

This photograph shows Neville Chamberlain and Adolf Hitler leaving the hotel in which discussions took place over the fate of Czechoslovakia at Bad Godesberg in September 1938.

appeared that all the obstacles in the way of a peaceful solution to the Czech crisis had been surmounted by Chamberlain's energetic shuttle diplomacy. On 22 September 1938, Chamberlain flew back to Germany to meet Hitler at the picturesque Rhineland town of Bad Godesberg. At the meeting, Chamberlain listened in utter amazement as Hitler flatly rejected the Anglo-French plan and outlined a set of further aggressive demands (dubbed the 'Godesberg memorandum'). Hitler now wanted German troops to occupy the Sudeten areas immediately, even demanding that non-German-speakers living there who wanted to leave could take only a suitcase of belongings with them. The single meagre concession Chamberlain wrung out of Hitler at the Godesberg summit was a promise to delay the military occupation of the Sudeten region until 1 October 1938. However, as Hitler had always planned to attack Czechoslovakia on this date anyway, it was hardly a great concession. Not surprisingly, the meeting at Godesberg ended in deadlock. Chamberlain returned to Britain in a deeply pessimistic mood.

Chamberlain was quite prepared to accept even the brutal terms of the Godesberg memorandum in order to find a peaceful resolution to the Czech crisis, but he was overruled by the cabinet, the French government, the Czecho-slovakians and British public opinion. It now seemed that the Czech crisis would result in the outbreak of a Second World War. Chamberlain's own attitude to the idea of going to war to save Czechoslovakia was quite graphically revealed in a live BBC radio broadcast on 27 September 1938, when he told listeners: 'How horrible, fantastic, incredible it is, that we should be . . . trying on gas masks here because of a quarrel in a far-away country between people of whom we know nothing'.

The Munich agreement

In a final desperate attempt to prevent war, Chamberlain asked Mussolini to persuade Hitler to settle the matter peacefully at a European conference. Meanwhile, leading German generals, fearful of a war breaking out on two fronts – against Britain and France in western Europe and the Soviet Union in the east – put strong pressure on Hitler to agree to a negotiated settlement. All this pressure worked: Hitler decided to settle the question by negotiation at a conference in Munich. The hastily convened Munich conference took place on the night of 29–30 September 1938, at the Brown House – the headquarters of the Nazi Party – in the Bavarian capital. It was attended by Hitler (for Germany), Chamberlain (for Britain), Édouard Daladier (for France) and Mussolini (for Italy). The Czechoslovak government was left outside the conference, while the Soviet Union was not even invited to attend.

The Munich conference simply agreed to the Sudetenland being incorporated into Nazi Germany by 10 October 1938. A vague promise was inserted into the agreement (which was never formally ratified) that all four signatories would respect the independence of the remainder of Czechoslovakia. The transfer of the Sudeten German areas was supposed to take place under international supervision, but was implemented by German troops in a very brutal fashion. Indeed, Germany gained more territory during the implementation of the Munich

WHAT, NO CHAIR FOR ME?

This cartoon (by David Low) warns of the possible adverse implications of leaving Stalin out of the discussions over the fate of Czechoslovakia during September 1938.

agreement than had been asked for by Hitler at Godesberg. The Munich conference was a return to old European diplomacy of the pre-1914 imperial variety, with a small country, without the military power to resist, being forced to concede territory to a more powerful European nation, with the approval of a number of other powerful European nations. Munich deprived Czechoslovakia of 70 per cent of its electricity power plants, and iron and steel factories, nearly all of its chemical works and its heavily fortified underground border defences along the German border.

The aftermath of Munich

Hitler was dissatisfied with the Munich agreement, even though it apparently gave him everything he wanted without firing a single shot. The reason for Hitler's anger was simple: he had wanted to crush Czechoslovakia by military force. He told a close associate: 'That senile old rascal Chamberlain has prevented my entry into Prague'. In a separate meeting which took place on 30 September 1938, Chamberlain persuaded Hitler to sign a piece of paper which declared that Britain and Germany were pledged 'never to go to war with one another again'. Chamberlain flourished this piece of paper (grandly dubbed the 'Anglo-German declaration') to the waiting newsreel cameramen and press reporters at Heston airport on his triumphant return from Munich. To Hitler, however, the notorious 'piece of paper' was a worthless promise, which he had no intention of keeping.

In spite of its dubious morality, the Munich agreement was a triumph for Chamberlain's bold new policy of appeasement. It had solved a major German grievance left behind by the Treaty of Versailles without a major European war. Yet the arguments over the wisdom of signing the Munich agreement have raged ever since. Winston Churchill predicted that Munich would come to be viewed as 'the blackest page in British history'. It is, in fact, very difficult to defend Munich on moral grounds. British policy throughout the Czech crisis was based on a selfish definition of what was best for British national interests, and ignored the broader moral question of whether it was right to force a small democratic nation to hand over territory to a brutal dictator. Put this way, Munich can be viewed as a major defeat for democratic principles in the settlement of international disputes.

On the other hand, it can be suggested that Britain was not prepared for war in 1938 and that Munich gained valuable time for Britain in which to improve its air defences, thereby enabling the RAF to survive the German air assaults during the later Battle of Britain. Munich can also be defended on the grounds that it offered Hitler one final opportunity to settle his remaining grievances by peaceful negotiation. If Hitler spurned this opportunity, it would be crystal clear that his ultimate aim was to dominate Europe by force. It should also be added that there was great public euphoria following the signing of the Munich agreement.

In the final analysis, the arguments against Munich are much stronger than those in favour. To begin with, the diplomatic negotiations which took place between Chamberlain and Hitler in September 1938 revealed that the Nazi dictator listened only to force. Even worse, the weakness displayed by Britain and France in accommodating Hitler's demands during the Czech crisis encouraged the Nazi dictator to push ahead with further bullying of small nations. In broader strategic terms, the signing of the Munich agreement was a disaster. If a European war had broken out in 1938, Hitler would have been forced to fight Britain, France, Czechoslovakia and the Soviet Union simultaneously on two fronts. The Munich agreement also greatly soured Stalin's attitude towards France and Britain, and thus sowed the seeds for the eventual signing of the Nazi–Soviet Pact in August 1939. Indeed, the extra year gained by Munich helped Germany far more than Britain and France. German war production was at a much higher level in 1939 than it had been in 1938, and the incorporation of the Sudetenland added vital new economic and military resources to the German war chest. More importantly, the extra year allowed Hitler to persuade Stalin to reject working with the western democracies and to remain a non-participant when France and Britain declared war on Germany in September 1939.

It seems that Chamberlain was determined for Munich to be viewed not as a bloodless victory for Nazi bullying, but as a personal triumph for his own passionate faith in the policy of appeasing the dictators. The famous piece of paper which Chamberlain waved so enthusiastically above his head on his arrival back in Britain was a further means of emphasising to the British public that the goal of preventing war through the policy of appeasement was of greater importance than the defence of a small power that was being bullied into submission by an obvious aggressor.

The period of hope

4.1 The Halifax visit: Chamberlain's view

The German visit was from my point of view a great success because it achieved its object, that of creating an atmosphere in which it is possible to discuss with Germany the practical questions involved in a European settlement . . . Both Hitler and Göring said separately, and emphatically, that they had no desire or intention of making war, and I think we may take this as correct, at any rate for the present. Of course they want to dominate Eastern Europe; they want as close a union with Austria as they can get without incorporating her in the Reich, and they want much the same things for the Sudetendeutsche as we did for the Uitlanders in the Transvaal . . . I think they [the Germans] would be prepared to come back to the League, if it were shorn of its compulsory powers, now clearly shown to be ineffective, and though Hitler was rather non-committal about disarmament, he did declare himself in favour of the abolition of bombing airplanes. Now here, it seems to me, is a fair basis of discussion, though no doubt all these points bristle with difficulties. But I don't see why we shouldn't say to Germany 'give us satisfactory assurances that you won't use force to deal with the Austrians and Czechoslovakians, and we will give you similar assurances that we won't use force to prevent the changes you want, if you can get them by peaceful means'.

Source: Neville Chamberlain papers, Chamberlain to Ida Chamberlain, 26 November 1937, Birmingham University Library (NC–18/1)

4.2 Chamberlain doubts whether the Foreign Office supports the appeasement of Mussolini

I am not too happy about the FO [Foreign Office] which seems to have no imagination and no courage . . . it is wearying to have always to begin at the beginning again and sometimes even to rewrite their dispatches for them. I am terribly afraid lest we should let the Anglo-Italian situation slip back to where it was before I intervened. The FO persists in seeing Musso only as a sort of Machiavelli putting on a false mask of friendship in order to further nefarious ambition. If we treat him like that we are going to get nowhere with him.

Source: Neville Chamberlain papers, 12 September 1937, Birmingham University Library (18/1/102)

4.3 A cabinet colleague offers an assessment of Chamberlain's approach to foreign policy

I had sympathy with Chamberlain's attitude . . . There was no certainty of war. He [Chamberlain] himself hated the idea of it. So, he believed, did all sensible men. Mussolini and Hitler must surely be sensible men too or they would never have risen to the great positions they occupied. Therefore they could not want war. There were certain things they did want, and there were certain things that we could give them. If he [Chamberlain] were in control of foreign policy, he could meet these men around a table and come to terms with them. The danger of war would be removed and we could get on with social reform. Chamberlain had many good qualities, but lacked the experience of the world . . . the continent of Europe was for him a closed book. He had been a successful Lord Mayor of Birmingham, and for him the Dictators of Germany and Italy were like the Lord Mayors of Liverpool and Manchester, who might belong to different political parties and have different interests, but who must desire the welfare of humanity, and be fundamentally reasonable decent men like himself. This profound misconception lay at the root of his policy and explains his mistakes.

Source: A. D. Cooper, *Old men forget: the autobiography of Alfred Duff Cooper*, London, 1954, p. 200

4.4 Anthony Eden's letter of resignation, February 1938

I have become increasingly conscious, as I know you [Chamberlain] have also, of a difference in outlook between us in respect to the international problems of the day and as to the methods by which we seek to resolve them. It cannot be in the country's interest that those who are called upon to direct its affairs should work in an uneasy partnership, fully conscious of differences in outlook yet hoping they will not recur. This applies with special force to the relationship between the Prime Minister and the Foreign Secretary.

Source: Cabinet papers, 20 February 1938, Public Record Office (CAB 23/92), London

4.5 Chamberlain outlines British policy in the aftermath of the union between Germany and Austria, March 1938

His Majesty's Government have expressed the view that recent events in Austria have created a new situation, and we think it right to state the conclusions to which consideration of these events has led us . . . There has been a profound disturbance of international confidence. In these circumstances the problem before Europe, to which in the opinion of His Majesty's Government it is their most urgent duty to direct their attention, is how best to restore this shaken confidence, how to maintain the rule of law, how to seek peaceful solutions to questions that continue to cause anxiety. Of these the one which is necessarily most present to many minds is that which concerns the relations between the Government of Czechoslovakia and the German minority in that country; and it is probable that a solution to this question, if it could be achieved, would go far to re-establish a sense of stability over an area much wider than that immediately concerned . . . So far as Czechoslovakia is concerned, it seems to His Majesty's

Government that now is the time when all the resources of diplomacy should be enlisted in the cause of peace . . . In the meantime, there is no need to assume the use of force, or, indeed, to talk about it. Such talk is to be strongly deprecated. Not only can it do no good; it is bound to do harm. It will interfere with the progress of diplomacy, and it must increase feelings of insecurity and uncertainty.

Source: *The Times*, 25 March 1938

4.6 Chamberlain's report of his first meeting with Hitler, Berchtesgaden, September 1938

I said I saw considerable practical difficulties about the secession of the Sudeten Germans . . . Even if, for example, the areas containing 80% of Germans were taken into the Reich, there would still be a considerable number of Germans left outside it, and, moreover, there would be a considerable number of Czechoslovakians in the German area and, therefore, it looks as though a solution . . . would require a change of boundaries . . . He [Hitler] said the percentages of Germans could not come into this. Where the Germans are in a majority the territory ought to pass to Germany . . . So far as he [Chamberlain] was concerned he didn't give two hoots whether the Sudetens were in the Reich or out of it.

Source: 'Account of conversation between Chamberlain and Hitler', 15 September 1938, Public Record Office (1/266), London

4.7 A leading Foreign Office official records his views of the Godesberg memorandum, September 1938

Hitler's memo, now in. It's awful. A week ago when we moved (or were pushed) from autonomy [for the Sudeten Germans] to cession, many of us found great difficulty in the idea of ceding people to Nazi Germany. We salved our consciences (at least I did) by stipulating it must be an 'orderly' secession – i.e. under international supervision, with safeguards for exchange of populations, compensation . . . Now Hitler says he must march into the whole area at once (to keep order) and the safeguards – and plebiscites! Can be held after! This is throwing away every safeguard that we had. PM [Prime Minister] is transmitting this 'proposal' to Prague. Thank God he hasn't yet recommended it for acceptance . . . Meeting of 'Inner Cabinet' at 3.30 p.m. and PM made his report to us. I was completely horrified – he [Chamberlain] was quite calmly for total surrender. More horrified still to find that Hitler has evidently hypnotized him to a point . . . I know we are in no position to fight; but I'd rather be beat than dishonoured. How can we look any foreigner in the face after this?

Source: D. Dilks (ed.), *The diaries of Alexander Cadogan*, London, 1971, pp. 103–04

4.8 Chamberlain broadcasts to the nation on BBC radio on the Czech crisis, 27 September 1938

I would not hesitate to pay even a third visit to Germany if I thought it would do any good . . . I am myself a man of peace to the depths of my soul. Armed conflict between nations is a nightmare to me; but if I was convinced that any nation had made up its mind to dominate the world by fear of its force I should feel it must be resisted. Under such a domination life for people who believe in liberty would not be worth living; but war is a fearful thing, and we must be very clear, before we embark on it, that it is really the great issues that are at stake.

Source: BBC radio broadcast by Chamberlain, quoted in *The Times*, 28 September 1938

4.9 The Munich conference: report of Sir Horace Wilson, Chamberlain's personal adviser, September 1938

It began with a statement by Herr Hitler thanking those present for their acceptance of his invitations and pointing out the need for speedy decisions . . . Mussolini said that he thought the best way of making progress was for someone to produce the basis for discussion, and he therefore read his Memorandum. It was evident that this document was a reasonable re-statement of much that had been discussed in the Anglo-French and the Anglo-German conversations and the Prime Minister was ready to accept it as a basis of discussion by the Conference . . . In the course of this discussion the Prime Minister raised the question of the representation at the Conference of the Czech Government. The conclusion was reached that the heads of the four powers [Britain, Germany, France and Italy] must accept responsibility for deciding – in the circumstances – how the situation should be dealt with . . . The German proposals for evacuation and occupation surprised us by their moderation . . . After very long delays due to inefficient organisation and lack of control, the Agreement and supplementaries were signed a little before 2 a.m. on the 30th September and the proceedings concluded by brief expressions of satisfaction.

Source: Sir Horace Wilson's note on the Munich conference, quoted in L. Butler and H. Jones (eds), *Britain in the twentieth century: a documentary reader*, London, 1994, p. 323

4.10 The 'Anglo-German declaration' signed by Hitler and Chamberlain, September 1938

We, the German Führer and Chancellor and the British Prime Minister, have had a meeting today and are agreed in recognising that the question of Anglo-German relations is of the first importance for the two countries and for Europe. We regard the agreement signed last night [the Munich agreement], and the Anglo-German Naval Agreement as symbolic of the desire of our two peoples never to go to war with one another again. We are resolved that the method of consultation shall be the method adopted to deal with any other questions that may concern our two countries, and we are determined to continue our efforts to remove possible sources of difference and thus contribute to assure the peace of Europe.

Source: N. Chamberlain, *The struggle for peace*, London, 1939, p. 189

4.11 Winston Churchill's view of the Munich agreement, October 1938

No one has been a more resolute and uncompromising struggler for peace than the Prime Minister. Everyone knows that. Never has there been such intense and undaunted determination to maintain and secure peace. Nevertheless, I am not quite clear why there was so much danger of Great Britain or France being involved in a war with Germany at this juncture if in fact they were ready all along to sacrifice Czechoslovakia. The terms which the Prime Minister brought back with him could easily have been agreed, I believe, through the ordinary diplomatic channels at any time during the summer. And I will say this, that I believe the Czechs, left to themselves, and told they were going to get no help from the Western Powers, would have been able to make better terms than they have got after all this tremendous perturbation. They could hardly have done worse. All is over. Silent, mournful, abandoned, broken, Czechoslovakia receded into darkness . . . I find unendurable the sense of our country falling into the German orbit and influence of Nazi Germany, and of our existence becoming dependent upon their good will or pleasure . . . I do not grudge our loyal, brave people, who were ready to do their duty no matter what the cost, who never flinched under the strain of last week, the natural, spontaneous outburst of joy and relief when they learned that the hard ordeal would no longer be required of them at the moment; but they should know the truth. They should know there has been gross neglect and deficiency in our defences; they should know that we have suffered a defeat without a war, the consequences of which will travel with us along our road; they should know we have passed an awful milestone in our history, when the whole equilibrium of Europe has been deranged . . . This is only the beginning of the reckoning. This is only the first sip, the first foretaste of a bitter cup which will be proffered to us year by year unless, by a supreme recovery of vigour, we rise again and take our stand for freedom as in the olden time.

Source: W. Churchill, *The gathering storm*, London, 1948, pp. 294–95

Document case-study questions

1 Outline the negotiating stance towards Germany implied by 4.1.

2 How useful is 4.2 as evidence of Chamberlain's attitude towards the Foreign Office?

3 What opinion of Chamberlain's approach to diplomacy does Cooper offer in 4.3?

4 Describe the basic point Eden is making about his relationship with Chamberlain in 4.4.

5 How is Chamberlain proposing to solve the Sudeten problem in 4.5?

6 According to 4.6, what is Chamberlain's underlying attitude towards the Sudeten Germans?

7 Does 4.7 provide any insights into Chamberlain's attitude towards the Godesberg memorandum?

8 In 4.8, how does Chamberlain choose to portray the plight of Czechoslovakia to the British public?

9 What can be learned from 4.9 about how the Munich conference was organised?

10 What might have been Chamberlain's motive for getting Hitler to sign the declaration outlined in 4.10?

11 Do you find 4.11 a convincing attack on the Munich agreement?

5 Chamberlain and appeasement (2): the road to war, October 1938–September 1939

STILL HOPE

Chamberlain is depicted in this cartoon as a 'dove of peace' in his negotiations with Hitler during the Czech crisis of 1938.

There was initially great euphoria over the Munich agreement. Chamberlain received over 20,000 letters and telegrams of congratulation. The cheers of the crowds in the aftermath of Munich were symbolic of the yearning of the British people to avoid a Second World War. Yet the initial optimism which accompanied the Munich agreement did not last very long.

The backlash against the Munich agreement

Shortly after the excitement had died down, the criticism began. Alfred Duff Cooper, the first lord of the admiralty, resigned from the cabinet in protest over the sacrifice of Czechoslovakia. Churchill described the Munich agreement as 'the blackest page in British history'. This assessment was shared by the great majority of Labour and Liberal MPs and by 30 rebel Conservatives, including Eden. Within Chamberlain's cabinet, which had previously been loyal to the policy of appeasement, there were many vocal demands made for a rapid acceleration of the rearmament programme. Halifax, the foreign secretary, made it plain to Chamberlain only days after Munich that he now regarded Hitler as a 'criminal lunatic' whose word could not be trusted. After Munich, therefore, Chamberlain's policy was subject to much greater criticism than ever before.

Public reaction to Munich

It is extremely difficult to accurately assess the reaction of ordinary members of the public towards Munich. It must be appreciated that a great deal of news management was undertaken by the Chamberlain government throughout the Czech crisis. No indication at all was given on BBC radio or by the cinema newsreels about the pressure and coercion which Chamberlain had exerted on the Czech government. Indeed, Chamberlain's famous return from Munich, when he waved the 'Anglo-German declaration' above his head in vainglorious triumph, was designed to give the impression of Hitler being in favour of lasting peace in Europe when, in all his private meetings with Chamberlain, Hitler had revealed himself as a completely unreasonable bully. It is probably worth adding that Chamberlain admitted to his private secretary that Hitler was 'the nastiest piece of work I have ever met', a view he did not communicate to the cabinet, to parliament or to the public.

During the Czech crisis, an organisation called Mass-Observation examined public opinion on appeasement. Mass-Observation used a national panel of 2,000 volunteers, who listened to the views of people on the Czech crisis, at home, at work and in pubs and social clubs. These observations revealed that most people had very little knowledge of the issues at stake. Indeed, most of those interviewed by Mass-Observation felt they had been kept completely in the dark by the British government during the Czech crisis. They were especially critical of the high level of secrecy surrounding the Munich negotiations. There was general support for Chamberlain's first visit to see Hitler at Berchtesgaden, but most people were 'very indignant' on hearing of the brutal terms asked of the Czechs in the Godesberg memorandum.

A national opinion poll taken shortly after the signing of the Munich agreement showed 51 per cent of the public 'satisfied' with the settlement, with 39 per cent 'not satisfied'. However, another opinion poll showed that 86 per cent of the population did not believe that the incorporation of the Sudetenland into the Third Reich represented Hitler's 'last territorial demands in Europe'. In fact, most people thought Munich had achieved merely a short postponement of a major European war.

Chamberlain's continuing confidence in appeasement

In the weeks after the Munich conference, Chamberlain remained surprisingly upbeat about the prospects for peace in Europe. He believed Munich had opened up the possibility of reaching further agreements with the dictators leading to a general settlement of European problems. Chamberlain dismissed those critics of appeasement inside and outside the cabinet who thought Munich had bought only a short breathing space in Hitler's timetable for war.

Increased armament

In October 1938, a majority of the cabinet, strongly supported by the military chiefs, pressed Chamberlain to increase war preparations. As a result, spending on rearmament increased from £1.5 billion to £2.1 billion in the aftermath of Munich, with the bulk of new expenditure devoted to the building of fighter aircraft. In fact, from the signing of the Munich agreement in September 1938 to the outbreak of war in September 1939, British spending on rearmament grew from 8.1 per cent of gross national product to 21.4 per cent.

Hitler's reaction to Munich

In Nazi Germany, Hitler was very sombre and depressed. After all, he had wanted to invade Czechoslovakia by force all along and regarded Munich as a humiliating climb-down. A mere three weeks after signing the agreement, he issued a directive to his generals ordering them to make all the necessary preparations to invade the remainder of Czechoslovakia.

Hitler's public speeches struck a distinctly anti-British tone after Munich. On 6 November 1938, Hitler claimed in a keynote speech that he would not be halted in his firm determination to press further 'legitimate' German claims by an 'umbrella-carrying British statesman' (this was an obvious reference to Chamberlain, who was always seen carrying an umbrella in public during his meetings with Hitler).

Difficulties with further appeasement

Nazi brutality against the Jews

On 9 November 1938, the Nazis launched a terrifying night of anti-Semitic thuggery throughout Germany (dubbed *Kristallnacht*), in which hundreds of Jewish-owned shops were set on fire and had their windows smashed. On that same dreadful 'night of broken glass', many Jewish synagogues were also burnt down. At the same time, Jews were attacked, arrested and killed. Most of the civilised world was outraged. The idea of appeasing such an openly brutal dictatorship seemed the height of folly and moral bankruptcy. Under strong pressure from the cabinet, the Church of England, most leading politicians and British public opinion, Chamberlain was forced to concede that undertaking political discussions with the Nazi regime had to be shelved for the foreseeable future.

Appeasing Mussolini

Yet Chamberlain refused to abandon the policy of appeasement completely. In order to keep some momentum going in the policy, he decided to pursue friendly relations with Europe's other famous fascist dictator, Mussolini. In January 1939, therefore, Chamberlain made a high-profile visit to Italy, accompanied by Halifax. He still cherished the hope that Hitler might be persuaded by Mussolini to moderate his demands. During the visit, however, Mussolini told Chamberlain he could not restrain Hitler from further foreign-policy adventures. Even so, Chamberlain, greatly heartened by the positive reception he had received from the Italian people during the visit, returned home in a very optimistic frame of mind about the policy of appeasement.

Hitler's next move in Europe

When he arrived home, Chamberlain was faced with a growing in-tray of gloomy intelligence reports which predicted that Hitler was planning to launch yet another foreign-policy adventure. One report suggested the Nazi dictator intended to mount an unprovoked military assault on Holland. Another gave evidence of plans for a German occupation of the remainder of Czechoslovakia, to be followed with further assaults on Poland and the Soviet Union. One intelligence source in Germany informed the British government that Hitler was even considering a lightning air attack on Britain.

In the light of these terrible predictions, the majority of the cabinet, supported eagerly by the military chiefs, pressed Chamberlain to make a firm public commitment to defend France, the strongest power in western Europe, from a German assault. On 6 February 1939, Chamberlain, reluctantly bowing to this pressure, announced that any threat to the vital interests of France in any part of the world would bring about immediate British intervention. Talks between British and French generals were also undertaken for the first time during the inter-war period. Finally, it was announced that the British Expeditionary Force would be greatly expanded in order to aid the French army in the event of war. These announcements amounted to the declaration of an Anglo-French alliance.

The occupation of Czechoslovakia

On 15 March 1939, German tanks suddenly entered Prague, ending what remained of the extremely fragile independence of Czechoslovakia. The Nazi takeover of Czechoslovakia destroyed the Munich agreement, wounded Chamberlain's reputation and mortally wounded the policy of appeasement. It revealed that diplomatic agreements signed with the Nazi dictator were worthless. It was no longer credible to argue, as Chamberlain had done, that Hitler's foreign-policy aims were exclusively linked to a revision of the Treaty of Versailles. On the contrary, it became generally accepted that Hitler fully intended to dominate Europe by military force unless he was halted.

It is, therefore, tempting to identify the occupation of Czechoslovakia as the point at which Chamberlain abandoned the policy of appeasement. However, the events which followed imply a more complex picture. Hitler's flagrant destruction of the Munich agreement did cause a great loss of confidence in Chamberlain's previously upbeat view that the Nazi dictator could be successfully appeased. However, Chamberlain did not alter his underlying belief that peaceful negotiation was a much better means of solving international difficulties than war. Indeed, he still remained hopeful that war might be averted – so long as Hitler was not antagonised.

The foreign-policy options facing Chamberlain after Prague

There appeared to be only three options left to the British government to deal with the aggression of Nazi Germany after the occupation of Prague:

1 to form a military alliance consisting of Britain, France, the Soviet Union and Poland (the last being the most likely next victim of Nazi aggression);
2 to create a broader group of powers, operating through the League of Nations, to halt further German aggression;
3 for Britain and France to offer firm support to defend Poland in the event of a German attack.

Of these three options, the most favoured one (especially among the British public) was the formation of an alliance with the Soviet Union. This move would have re-created the pre-1914 Triple Entente. The attraction of a French–British–Soviet alliance was that it might deter Hitler from attacking Poland, but even if it did not it would force Germany to fight a war on two military fronts. This would be likely to prove a lengthy war of attrition: the very type of war for which the German army (and the German economy) was not prepared.

The creation of a broader group of powers, although it would have extended the number of enemies which Germany would face in war, appeared less attractive, primarily because the League of Nations had lost a great deal of credibility. The least popular option was for Britain and France to offer a guarantee to defend Poland from a German attack, without any aid from either the Soviet Union or other members of the League of Nations. Winston Churchill, one of the leading critics of appeasement, suggested that a guarantee to Poland was unlikely to deter Hitler, as Britain and France had given a similar guarantee to Czechoslovakia at Munich, which they had not upheld. A simple glance at the map of Europe showed another severe flaw in the idea of an Anglo-French guarantee to Poland: it was worthless without Soviet military help. Moreover, the Polish army, acting alone, stood no chance of resisting the modern and well-equipped German army.

The guarantee to Poland

Yet Chamberlain opted for a guarantee to Poland on 31 March 1939 (this was quickly supported by the French government). The timing of the Polish guarantee was due to intelligence reports suggesting that Hitler might invade Poland. These concerns were not unjustified. After all, on 21 March 1939 Hitler had demanded the return of Danzig from Poland, and on 23 March German troops had marched into occupied Memel (which had been seized from Germany by Lithuania in 1923). The guarantee to Poland appeared to set a limit on Anglo-French toleration of any further German expansion in eastern Europe. It was designed to

The territorial expansion of Nazi Germany, 1936–39.

warn Hitler of the determination of Britain and France to go to war in the event of Germany launching a military attack on Poland. Yet the actual wording of the guarantee referred to a British commitment to 'uphold the independence of the Polish state' without making any mention of defending Poland's existing borders.

In April 1939, Britain and France offered equally ambiguous guarantees to Romania, Greece and Turkey, which were accepted, and made similar offers to Holland, Switzerland and Denmark, but these nations rejected them. In theory, the Anglo-French guarantees were designed to act as deterrents to further

German aggression. In practice, it was difficult for Hitler to take them seriously: he was firmly convinced they would not be honoured.

It is also important to emphasise that the British guarantee to Poland was not followed up by any substantial economic or military aid to the Polish government. In April 1939, for example, the Polish government asked Chamberlain for a loan of £60 million to purchase vital military equipment in order to meet the expected German attack, but all the Poles were offered was a £5 million bank credit, which was to be made available only if the sum was matched by the French government (which it was not). In essence, the British and French governments were not only incapable of defending Poland, but they were not even prepared to provide the substantial sums needed for Poland to defend itself from a German attack.

Chamberlain's reasons for offering the guarantee

It seems that four important factors underlay Chamberlain's decision to offer the guarantee to Poland:

1 a fear of further German aggression in eastern Europe;
2 the Polish government had indicated it preferred a guarantee from France and Britain to any involvement by the Soviet Union;
3 a Polish guarantee allowed Chamberlain to pursue a policy of deterrence against Nazi Germany without the extreme provocation which he believed an alliance with the Soviet Union involved;
4 a guarantee might induce Hitler to seek Anglo-German negotiation over the Danzig question.

The British guarantee to Poland was, therefore, a middle way between appeasement, which seemed no longer possible given Hitler's obvious desire for aggression, and the creation of an anti-Hitler alliance. To have opted for such an alliance would have been a definite abandonment of appeasement, which Chamberlain was not prepared to contemplate, even though it would have signalled a clear determination to halt Hitler's march across eastern Europe.

The response of Hitler and Mussolini to the guarantee

Hitler was completely unmoved by the Anglo-French guarantee to Poland. On 3 April 1939, he ordered his leading generals to prepare plans for a military attack on Poland (code named Operation White), provisionally set to begin at any time from 1 September 1939. A few days later, Hitler announced he would no longer be bound by the terms of the 1935 Anglo-German naval agreement.

Mussolini's actions in the weeks following the Anglo-French announcement of the guarantee to Poland showed that the Italian dictator did not take the belated Anglo-French show of strength seriously either. On 7 April 1939, Italian troops occupied Albania, a small country neither Britain nor France had bothered to guarantee. On 22 May 1939, Mussolini and Hitler signed a military alliance, dubbed the 'Pact of Steel', which added further to the general feeling that war in Europe was moving ever closer.

The search for an alliance with the Soviet Union

It was quickly recognised by everyone (with the possible exception of Chamberlain and his most blinkered remaining supporters) that the guarantee system was not working, because the dictators were still engaging in acts of unprovoked aggression against small powers and promising more of the same in the very near future. The only feasible way of preventing Hitler's highly predictable attack on Poland was for Britain and France to sign (and pretty quickly) a military alliance with the Soviet Union, without quibbling too much about the small print. Indeed, very strong pressure was placed on Chamberlain from the majority of MPs, the military chiefs and public opinion to follow this course of action. Yet Chamberlain quite stubbornly continued to cast doubt on the need for such an alliance and continued to put up a number of objections:

1. he did not have any faith in Soviet military power;
2. he did not trust Stalin;
3. he disliked communism.

Yet the most important reason why Chamberlain put obstacles in the way of signing an alliance with the Soviet Union was that such an arrangement spelled a definite end to the policy of appeasing Hitler. It would have ended his underlying hope of somehow reviving Anglo-German negotiations for a peaceful settlement of the Danzig issue. It is probably worth adding that Chamberlain did not want to admit that his policy of appeasement was flawed and that his critics – particularly Churchill – were right. Hence, he obstinately refused to accept the logic of his opponents.

By the end of May 1939, however, such was the weight of political pressure on Chamberlain that negotiations designed to bring about an alliance with the Soviet Union were put in motion. Yet Chamberlain still remained deeply sceptical as to whether such an alliance was the key to preventing the outbreak of a Second World War. He believed Hitler would be so outraged by the signing of a British–French–Soviet alliance that he would not contemplate entering into any negotiations with Poland over the Danzig question, but would rather launch a military attack. He still clung on to a powerful underlying belief that Germany and Poland might resolve their differences by negotiation, if the Soviet Union could be kept out of the picture. Even if Chamberlain was not cold-bloodedly planning a second Munich for his newly found Polish friends (about whom he knew next to nothing), his mind was working in the same blinkered way it had done during the prelude to Munich, except he no longer had the same degree of freedom to follow his own desired course of action, which was to bring about some kind of negotiated settlement between Germany and Poland.

The failure to gain an Anglo-Soviet alliance

In spite of the critical nature of the situation in Europe, the negotiations by the British government for an alliance with the Soviet Union went along at a surprisingly leisurely pace. On 18 April 1939, the Soviet Union offered to sign a three-power pact of mutual assistance with Britain and France, but the British government placed so many obstacles in the way of the Soviet proposal that it was not implemented.

On 23 July 1939 Chamberlain finally gave the go-ahead for direct negotiations with the Soviet Union in Moscow. The French government wanted a swift conclusion of a military alliance and found it difficult to understand why the British were nit-picking over the small print. Chamberlain (supported by Halifax) made no real effort to inject any urgency into the negotiations. The British diplomatic mission sent to the Soviet Union in the summer of 1939 was headed by a little-known admiralty figure, with a name as long-winded as the British negotiating stance: Sir Reginald Aylmer Ranfurly Plunkett-Ernle-Erle-Drax. He was accompanied by Sir William Strang, a relatively junior Foreign Office official. The British diplomatic mission travelled to Leningrad on 5 August 1939 on a merchant ship, which took six days to arrive.

Chamberlain did not even consider going to the Soviet Union, he refused to send Halifax (who, in any case, did not want to go) and he flatly rejected a rather friendly offer from Eden (a strong supporter of an Anglo-Soviet alliance) to conduct the negotiations. The leading Soviet diplomatic and military figures who greeted the British delegation on its arrival were surprised to learn that neither Drax nor Strang had been given the power by Chamberlain to sign an alliance, even if one was agreed there and then. To make matters worse, the British mission insisted that any alliance must be cloaked under the moribund covenant of the League of Nations.

Chamberlain did not seem to appreciate that the Soviet Union was in a very strong diplomatic position in the summer of 1939 and would sign an alliance on its own terms. Stalin wanted copper-bottomed guarantees from Britain and France that they would not wriggle out of any agreement. He also refused to give Britain and France any assurances about the future independence of Poland, Romania, Czechoslovakia or Finland. Not surprisingly, the talks in Moscow between Britain and France on the one side and the Soviet delegation on the other quickly reached complete deadlock when the Polish government refused to allow Soviet troops onto Polish soil in the event of a German attack.

The Nazi–Soviet pact

The bungled attempt by the British government to conclude a military alliance with the Soviet Union was a diplomatic disaster of the very highest order. It allowed Hitler (the supreme opportunist) to exploit the situation by offering Stalin a very attractive non-aggression pact (signed on 23 August 1939). The British government in general, and Chamberlain in particular, had deliberately stalled their own negotiations with the Soviet Union because they believed the ideological incompatibility between Hitler and Stalin, and National Socialism and Soviet communism, rendered a Nazi–Soviet pact impossible. What Chamberlain overlooked – and he should have known better given his personal experience of Hitler's actions during the Czech crisis – was this simple fact: Hitler was quite

DOUBTFUL FRIENDS

This *Punch* cartoon from September 1939 points out the possible adverse effects of the
Nazi–Soviet pact for the small nations of eastern Europe.

prepared to sign any piece of paper which would allow him to continue with his
foreign-policy objectives.

There has been a fierce historical debate over exactly when and for what
reasons Stalin finally abandoned the idea of forging an alliance with Britain and
France against Hitler and opted instead for a non-aggression pact with the Nazi
dictator. Of course, Stalin realised he was in a very strong diplomatic position
and he could not fathom why the British and French governments were haggling
with him over the details of the proposed alliance. He eventually concluded that
the British and the French governments were not really serious about standing
up to Nazi aggression and were conducting the negotiations to satisfy public
opinion in their own countries.

Some historians have attempted to build up a picture of Stalin cold-bloodedly
plotting a pact with his totalitarian alter ego: Hitler. Yet this argument is

unconvincing. If this were the case, then why did the Soviet Union originally offer to sign a military alliance with France and Britain in April 1939? It was the continual haggling over details, and the seemingly endless delay, which led Stalin to conclude by August 1939 that there was no enthusiasm or commitment on the British side to conclude an alliance. As a result, he saw no reason to engage his entire army in the defence of a Polish government that did not want his help and a British government that had consistently ignored and diplomatically marginalised the Soviet Union for most of the inter-war period.

It is Chamberlain who must shoulder the major share of the blame for the failure to gain an alliance with the Soviet Union. Chamberlain always believed a guarantee to Poland, although judged a very feeble deterrent by everyone else, offered the best prospect of finding a negotiated settlement of the German–Polish dispute, without an escalation of that conflict into a major European war. This explains why he was so unenthusiastic towards the whole idea of an Anglo-Soviet military alliance from beginning to end.

The outbreak of war

Hitler was firmly convinced that the signing of the Nazi–Soviet pact would lead swiftly to Poland being forced by Britain and France to accede to German demands. He was surprised, therefore, when Chamberlain publicly declared on 23 August 1939 that the British government fully intended to honour its obligations towards Poland. On 25 August 1939, the British government signed a formal military alliance with Poland. This display of firmness by Chamberlain came as something of a shock to Hitler, who decided it was a mere negotiating ploy by the 'cowardly' British prime minister. As a result, Hitler decided to delay his attack on Poland, which had been set for 26 August 1939.

In a further clear attempt to put in motion a 'second Munich', Hitler generously offered to Chamberlain a guarantee of the British empire in return for his help in finding a negotiated settlement of the Polish–German dispute over Danzig. Hitler asked the Polish leaders to come to Berlin to negotiate a settlement. Chamberlain communicated Hitler's request to the Polish government, but Polish ministers – much to Chamberlain's surprise and annoyance – refused to undertake any negotiations with the Nazi regime over the Danzig question. What Chamberlain never fully appreciated when he hastily offered a guarantee to Poland was that the Polish government, a nationalistic military-style dictatorship, was quite prepared to undertake a suicidal war with Nazi Germany rather than simply concede territory in humiliating circumstances as the Czechs had done after Munich. It was the Polish government, therefore, which killed off any chance of a second Munich-style agreement, because they preferred to fight Hitler's superior army rather than giving in without a struggle, as Czechoslovakia had done.

On 1 September 1939, Hitler, outraged at the steadfast refusal of the Poles to submit to his demands, gave the go-ahead for the German attack on Poland. Yet, for almost two long days, the British and French governments agonisingly

WANTED!

FOR MURDER . . . FOR KIDNAPPING . . . FOR THEFT AND FOR ARSON

ADOLF HITLER
ALIAS
Adolf Schicklegruber, Adolf Hittler or Hidler

Last heard of in Berlin, September 3, 1939. Aged fifty, height 5ft. 8½in., dark hair, frequently brushes one lock over left forehead. Blue eyes. Sallow complexion, stout build, weighs about 11st. 3lb. Suffering from acute monomania, with periodic fits of melancholia. Frequently bursts into tears when crossed. Harsh, guttural voice, and has a habit of raising right hand to shoulder level. DANGEROUS!

Can be recognised full face by habitual scowl. Rarely smiles Talks rapidly, and when angered screams like a child.

Profile from a recent photograph. Black moustache. Jowl inclines to fatness. Wide nostrils. Deep-set, menacing eyes.

FOR MURDER Wanted for the murder of over a thousand of his fellow countrymen on the night of the Blood Bath, June 30, 1934. Wanted for the murder of countless political opponents in concentration camps.

He is indicted for the murder of Jews, Germans, Austrians, Czechs, Spaniards and Poles. He is now urgently wanted for homicide against citizens of the British Empire.

Hitler is a gunman who shoots to kill. He acts first and talks afterwards. No appeals to sentiment can move him. This gangster, surrounded by armed hoodlums, is a natural killer. The reward for his apprehension, dead or alive, is the peace of mankind.

FOR KIDNAPPING Wanted for the kidnapping of Dr. Kurt Schuschnigg, late Chancellor of Austria. Wanted for the kidnapping of Pastor Niemoller, a heroic martyr who was not afraid to put God before Hitler. Wanted for the attempted kidnapping of Dr. Benes, late President of Czechoslovakia. The kidnapping tendencies of this established criminal are marked and violent. The symptoms before an attempt are threats, blackmail and ultimatums. He offers his victims the alternatives of complete surrender or timeless incarceration in the horrors of concentration camps.

FOR THEFT Wanted for the larceny of eighty millions of Czech gold in March, 1939. Wanted for the armed robbery of material resources of the Czech State. Wanted for the stealing of Memelland. Wanted for robbing mankind of peace, of humanity, and for the attempted assault on civilisation itself. This dangerous lunatic masks his raids by spurious appeals to honour, to patriotism and to duty. At the moment when his protestations of peace and friendship are at their most vehement, he is most likely to commit his smash and grab.

His tactics are known and easily recognised. But Europe has already been wrecked and plundered by the depredations of this armed thug who smashes by without scruple.

FOR ARSON Wanted as the incendiary who started the Reichstag fire on the night of February 27, 1933. This crime was the key point, and the starting signal for a series of outrages and brutalities that are unsurpassed in the records of criminal degenerates. As a direct and immediate result of this calculated act of arson, an innocent dupe, Van der Lubbe, was murdered in cold blood. But as an indirect outcome of this carefully-planned offence, Europe itself is ablaze. The fires that this man has kindled cannot be extinguished until he himself is apprehended—dead or alive!

THIS RECKLESS CRIMINAL IS WANTED—DEAD OR ALIVE!

All the above information has been obtained from official sources and has been collated by CASSANDRA

A page from the *Daily Mirror* (4 September 1939) pins the blame for starting the Second World War exclusively on Adolf Hitler.

delayed a formal declaration of war. Chamberlain turned to Mussolini in the hope that he might persuade Hitler to conclude a negotiated settlement of the German–Polish dispute. However, Mussolini's intervention came to nothing, primarily because the British and French insisted on a withdrawal of German troops from Poland as a precondition of any opening of talks.

If the Polish government had not proved so intransigent towards negotiating with Hitler over the Danzig question, then it seems more than likely that Chamberlain would have achieved a 'second Munich'. However, most British politicians and the majority of the British public may not have stomached this solution – and his government would probably have been forced out of office had he openly proposed such a solution. As a result, Chamberlain could not attempt to coerce the Poles in any way during the Danzig crisis. What he could and did do was delay the declaration of war for as long as possible, in order to get the Italian government to try to persuade Hitler to come to some kind of negotiated agreement. It was only when Chamberlain realised these negotiations would come to nothing that he finally accepted war had to be declared.

At 11 a.m. on 3 September 1939, Chamberlain announced on BBC radio that Britain was at war with Germany. He also admitted that all his efforts to maintain peace had 'crashed in ruins'. At 5 p.m. on the same fateful day, the French government also declared war on Nazi Germany.

Chamberlain had set out as prime minister to discover whether Hitler wanted a revision of the Treaty of Versailles or whether he aimed to dominate Europe by force. However, war came to Europe because Chamberlain took far too long to accept the logical answer to that question, namely that Hitler was all along hell bent on military aggression and had to be stopped by military force. The way in which Chamberlain went about trying to stop Hitler after the occupation of Prague involved taking measures which were always designed not to antagonise the Nazi dictator. As a result, he avoided signing military agreements which might have deterred Hitler and which would certainly have forced him to fight on two military fronts, one of which was a war of attrition with the Soviet Union – the very conflict the German army ultimately proved incapable of winning.

Document case study

The road to war

5.1 The Nazi occupation of Czechoslovakia: the view of a Conservative MP, March 1939

Hitler has entered Prague, apparently, and Czechoslovakia has ceased to exist. No bolder departure from the written bond has ever been committed in history. The manner of it surpasses comprehension and his [Hitler's] callous desertion of the Prime Minister [Chamberlain] is stupefying. I can never forgive him . . . The PM must be discouraged and horrified. He acceded to the demand of the Opposition for a debate and the business of the House was altered. Then he rose, and calmly, but I am sure with a broken heart, made a frank statement of the facts as he knew them . . . I thought he looked miserable. His whole policy of appeasement is in ruins. Munich is a torn up episode . . . The country is stirred to its depths, and rage against Germany is rising.

Source: R. James (ed.), *The diaries of Sir Henry 'Chips' Channon*, London, 1967, pp. 185–86

5.2 The Nazi occupation of Czechoslovakia: the view of Chamberlain, March 1939

Germany under its present regime has sprung a series of unpleasant surprises upon the world. The Rhineland, the Austria *Anschluss*, the severance of the Sudetenland – all these things shocked and affronted public opinion throughout the world. Yet however much we might take exception to the methods which were adopted in each of these cases, there was something to be said, whether on account of racial affinity or of just claims too long resisted . . . But the events which have taken place this past week in complete disregard of the principle laid down by the German Government itself seem to fall into a different category and must cause us all to be asking ourselves: Is this the end of the story, or is it the beginning of a new one? Is this the last attack on a small state, or is it to be followed by others? Is this, in fact, a step in the direction of an attempt to dominant the world by force?

Source: *The Times*, 18 March 1939

5.3 The British guarantee to Poland: statement by Chamberlain, April 1939

I now have to inform the House that in the event of any action which clearly threatened Polish independence, and which the Polish government accordingly considered it vital to resist with their national force, His Majesty's Government would feel themselves bound at once to lend the Polish government all support in their power. They have given the Polish government an assurance to this effect.

Source: *Parliamentary Debates (Hansard)*, 3 April 1939, cols 2482–85

5.4 Hitler speaks to the generals, May 1939

After six years the present situation is as follows: With minor exceptions German unification has been achieved. Further success cannot be achieved without bloodshed. Poland will always be on the side of our adversaries. Despite the friendship agreement Poland has always intended to exploit every opportunity against us. Danzig is not the objective. It is a matter of expanding our living space in the east, of making our food supplies secure, and of solving the problem of the Baltic states. To provide sufficient food you must have sparsely settled areas. This is fertile soil, whose surpluses will be very much increased by German management . . . There is therefore no question of sparing Poland, and the decision remains to attack Poland at the first suitable opportunity. We cannot expect a repetition of Czechoslovakia. There will be fighting. The task is to isolate Poland. Success in isolating her will be decisive. Therefore, the Führer must reserve to himself the final command to attack. There will be no simultaneous conflict with the West [France and Britain] . . . Basic principle: conflict with Poland, beginning with attack on Poland, will only be successful if the West keeps out. If that is impossible, then it is better to attack the West and finish off Poland at the same time. It will be the task of dexterous diplomacy to isolate Poland.

Source: *Documents on German foreign policy, Vol. 6*, London, 1956, no. 433

5.5 Chamberlain has doubts about the benefits of an Anglo-Soviet alliance, March 1939

I must confess to a most profound distrust of Russia. I have no belief whatever in her ability to maintain an effective offensive, even if she wanted to. And I distrust her motives which seem to me to have little connection with our ideas of liberty, and to be concerned only with getting everyone by the ears. Moreover, she is both hated and suspected by the smaller states, notably, Poland, Rumania and Finland.

Source: Chamberlain's diary, 26 March, quoted in K. Feiling, *The life of Neville Chamberlain*, London, 1946, p. 403

5.6 Hitler's speech to the generals, August 1939

Decision to attack Poland was arrived at in spring . . . Our strength lies in our quickness and in our brutality: Genghis Khan has sent millions of women and children into death knowingly and with a light heart. History sees him only as the great founder of States. As to what the weak western European civilisation asserts about me, that is of no account. I have given the command and I shall shoot everyone who utters a word of criticism, for the goal to be obtained in war is not that of reaching certain lines but of physically demolishing the opponent. As for the present only in the east I have put my death-head [an elite and brutal Nazi force] formation in place with the command . . . to send into death many women and children of Polish origin and language. Only thus can we gain the living space that we need . . . I experienced those poor worms Daladier and Chamberlain in Munich. They will be too cowardly to attack. They won't go beyond a blockade . . . Poland will be depopulated and settled with Germans. My pact with the Poles was merely conceived of as a gaining of time. As for the rest, gentlemen, the fate of Russia will be exactly the same as I am now going through in the case of Poland. After Stalin's death – he is a very sick man – we will break the Soviet Union. Then will begin the dawn of the German rule of the earth . . . Be hard, be without mercy, act more quickly and brutally than the others. The citizens of western Europe must tremble with horror. That is the most humane way of conducting a war. For it scares the other off.

Source: *Documents on British foreign policy, Vol. 7*, London, 1954, no. 314

5.7 Chamberlain explains the British delay in declaring war on Germany, September 1939

The final long-drawn-out agonies that preceded the actual declaration of war were as nearly unendurable as could be. We were anxious to bring matters to a head, but there were three complications – the secret communications that were going on with Goering and Hitler through a neutral intermediary, the conference proposal of Mussolini and the French anxiety to postpone the actual declaration as long as possible, until they could evacuate their women and children, and mobilise their armies. There was very little of this that we could say to the public, and meantime the House of Commons was out of hand, torn with suspicions . . . [some of them believing] the government guilty of cowardice and treachery . . . So the war began, after a short and troubled night, and only the fact that one's mind works at three times its ordinary pace on such occasions enabled me to get through my broadcast [on BBC radio, 3 September 1939, announcing 'Britain is at war with Germany'], the formation of the war Cabinet, the meeting of the House of Commons, and the preliminary orders on that awful Sunday, which the calendar tells me was this day a week ago.

Source: Chamberlain's diary, 10 September, quoted in K. Feiling, *The life of Neville Chamberlain*, London, 1946, pp. 416–17

Document case-study questions

1 Describe Chamberlain's attitude, as outlined in 5.1, towards the Nazi takeover of Czechoslovakia.

2 What does 5.2 tell us about Chamberlain's view of Hitler's aims in foreign policy?

3 Explain the significance of 5.3 for Britain's approach to the problems of eastern Europe.

4 Comment on the significance of 5.4 in establishing responsibility for the outbreak of the Second World War.

5 What does 5.5 tell us about Chamberlain's likely commitment to the signing of an Anglo-Soviet alliance?

6 Given Hitler's views as expressed in 5.6, what is your opinion of the likelihood that Hitler could have been successfully appeased?

7 Evaluate the reliability of 5.7 as evidence of Chamberlain's motives for delaying the declaration of war.

6 The historical debate

At the show trials of the leading surviving Nazi war criminals, held at Nuremberg at the end of the Second World War, Hitler and the Nazi regime were assigned primary responsibility for the outbreak of the war. However, the policy of appeasement has always been viewed by historians as among the important contributory factors to war breaking out. The aim of this concluding chapter is to examine the debate among historians surrounding the roles played by Hitler, Chamberlain and appeasement in the outbreak of the Second World War.

The Hitlocentric interpretation

There has been a protracted debate over the role played by the foreign-policy aims of Adolf Hitler in explaining the outbreak of the Second World War. The singularly most dominant view in this debate is that of Hugh Trevor Roper (later Lord Dacre), who argued that Hitler's foreign-policy actions from 1933 to 1939 were the implementation of a very carefully planned programme of aggression, laid out by Hitler in *Mein Kampf*, which had been completed while the Nazi leader was in Landsberg prison. According to Trevor Roper, Hitler's first objective was to gain *Lebensraum* (living space) for Germany in eastern Europe through a bloody war of military conquest against the Soviet Union. To achieve this ultimate goal, Hitler intended to move step by step, concentrating on the attainment of one objective at a time.

Another historian who supported the idea of Hitler following clearly defined aims in foreign policy was Alan Bullock, a leading British historian and the author of the most well known biography of the Nazi demagogue. However, Bullock modified Trevor Roper's interpretation in a very subtle manner by suggesting that the Nazi dictator's pursuit of his firm objective of *Lebensraum* was accompanied by opportunism in both the method and tactics used to carry out his foreign policy. Hitler attempted to shroud his aims in the language of sweet reason and would sign pacts and pledges he had no intention of keeping.

The idea of Hitler following a pre-existing plan in foreign policy, implemented in stages (known as the doctrine of 'limited objectives'), has been strongly endorsed in many subsequent studies. Klaus Hildebrand, for example, suggests Hitler was following a careful and premeditated 'stage by stage plan' (dubbed *Stufenplan*) in foreign policy, which had the gaining of *Lebensraum* in eastern Europe through a war of conquest in the Soviet Union as its primary objective. In the view of Andreas Hillgruber, Hitler was following a three-stage plan, involving the domination of Europe in the first instance, to be followed by gaining the territory and oil resources of the Middle East in its second stage, leading ultimately to an all-out war for world domination against the USA.

The supporters of the orthodox view of Hitler's foreign-policy aims, often dubbed the 'Hitlocentric interpretation' (or 'intentionalist view'), see Hitler as the dominant force in the decision-making process on German foreign affairs. According to Gerhard Weinberg, a leading German historian of foreign policy, the major decisions on foreign policy under Nazi rule were taken by Hitler. As soon as Hitler came to power, therefore, Germany was heading towards an unfolding programme of military aggression, which made war in Europe inevitable. The only realistic accommodation Chamberlain could have reached with Hitler, given his underlying objectives, was for the British government to abandon its age-old commitment to uphold the balance of power in Europe, thereby allowing the Nazi dictator a 'free hand' to achieve German domination of eastern Europe. In return, Hitler was prepared, in the short term at least, to tolerate the continuance of the British empire. The price of such an Anglo-German agreement, however, would have been a British acceptance of German domination of the continent of Europe.

The revisionist view

On the other side of the debate are the 'revisionist' historians (also known as 'structuralists'), who reject the view that Hitler's foreign policy was the direct outcome of a consistent 'master plan', executed stage by stage, albeit with a high level of tactical flexibility and improvisation. The most famous revisionist interpretation of Hitler's role in the origins of the Second World War was advanced by A. J. P. Taylor in his very controversial and thought-provoking study *The origins of the Second World War*, which was published in 1961. Taylor, writing with great flair and style, rejected the idea of Hitler as a systematic and clear-sighted planner, following a blueprint for European domination. Instead, Taylor viewed him as a master of improvisation and opportunism, with imprecise and constantly changing aims. Even more controversially, and probably mischievously, Taylor described Hitler as 'an ordinary German statesman', whose foreign policy was similar to that of previous German governments. Taylor did not even view Hitler as primarily responsible for the outbreak of the Second World War. On the contrary, he claimed that the real culprits for the international crisis of the 1930s were the peacemakers of 1919, who had failed to completely eradicate the possibility of a German military revival. Taylor viewed Chamberlain's determined bid to appease German grievances as a very realistic assessment of the failings of the past and a well-meaning attempt to solve them. According to Taylor, Munich was a triumph for appeasement because it solved a key German grievance and at least delayed the outbreak of a major European war. Indeed, Taylor claims that war came quickly in 1939 because Chamberlain, under pressure from his domestic critics, was forced – with some reluctance – to abandon appeasement without putting in place a carefully worked out alternative. In the view of Taylor, the abandonment of appeasement led Chamberlain into making some monumental errors, most notably the guarantee to Poland and the failure to secure an Anglo-Soviet agreement. Taylor claimed that Hitler did not want a European war to break out in September 1939 over his dispute with Poland and he would have gladly accepted 'a second Munich', if only it could have been arranged by Chamberlain. The Second World War broke out, according to Taylor, because the British and French governments were unwilling to coerce the 'intransigent' Polish government into meeting Hitler's demands and decided to meet force with force when neither country was in a strong enough military position to do so.

These extremely controversial views were roundly attacked when Taylor's book was first published, but some of his ideas are now treated much more seriously. In recent revisionist studies, it has become commonplace to assert that if Hitler had a master plan, which they doubt, it was capable of modification in the face of internal and external pressures. Karl Dietrich Bracher argues that Hitler's foreign-policy actions had no overall design, but were rather sponta-neous and unplanned responses to internal divisions within German society. In support of this view, Martin Broszat suggests there is very little evidence of systematic planning in most of Hitler's foreign-policy actions. In this respect, Broszat points to Hitler's apparent lack of a clear plan about the future of Poland for most of the 1930s, in spite of its important geographical location for his proposed attack on the Soviet Union. Indeed, Broszat suggests that many of Hitler's so-called crystal-clear aims were in reality mere Utopian dreams, not supported by co-ordinated planning.

In a similar vein, Wolfgang Schieder has shown that Hitler's foreign policy contained a dogmatic rigidity combined with such flexibility that it is very difficult to conclude it was simply the implementation of a pre-existing master plan. By and large, the revisionists have stressed the internal limitations on Hitler's freedom of action in foreign affairs from competing centres of power within big business, the bureaucracy, the Nazi elite and the army.

The economic pressure on the Nazi regime in the late 1930s has also been emphasised in some revisionist studies. Tim Mason has argued that the German decision to attack Poland in 1939 was related to the economic problems created by vast armament spending, which placed great pressure on the German economy. As a result, a short war with Poland was undertaken in order to acquire additional economic resources to prop up a faltering economy. David Kaiser has shown that each Nazi occupation from 1938 onwards injected vital new resources into the German economy, which helped to ward off recession. According to this view, the Nazi drive for self-sufficiency, combined with rapid rearmament, had created an economic situation in which short wars of economic plunder against small powers had become vital. However, the view that Hitler went to war because of economic pressure has not been accepted by everyone. Richard Overy has convincingly shown that the economic problems faced by Germany in the late 1930s did not require short wars of plunder to solve them. In the view of Overy, Hitler's decision to attack Poland was not determined

– or even greatly influenced – by economic factors, but was more due to power-political considerations. In fact, Romania, with its vital reserves of oil, was a much better economic target to solve Germany's immediate economic problems than impoverished Poland.

In spite of the extensive research undertaken by the revisionists, they have failed to disprove that Hitler's foreign policy was the consistent implementation of his aims in a stage-by-stage process. Klaus Hildebrand argues that the revisionists have repeatedly failed to show how Hitler's freedom of action in the foreign-policy arena was limited by domestic and economic factors. Ian Kershaw has claimed that, while Hitler took very little interest in resolving domestic and economic problems, the same was not true in the area of foreign policy, where the Nazi leader took all the most important decisions and often ignored advice from the army, the foreign ministry and the Nazi elite when deciding on a particular course of action.

Of course, Hitler's foreign policy did not operate completely free of domestic and international pressure. Even so, the greatest pressure on Hitler's actions emanated from the response of his potential enemies. In actual fact, Hitler's success in foreign policy, which resulted primarily from his bloodless victories over rearmament, the Rhineland, Austria and Czechoslovakia, served to increase his ability to take major decisions without regard to the views of internal opponents. His actions in foreign policy during the late 1930s had created such a critical situation that the Nazi dictator either had to push forward on the path of revising the existing European order by force, if necessary, which was the course on which he was set, or had to come to an agreed settlement of his grievances with the British and French governments. They had shown a great willingness to tolerate his actions and decided to set limits on German expansion only in March 1939 by means of the guarantee to Poland. By this time, Hitler was fully prepared to risk a war with Britain and France in order to achieve vast territorial gains for Germany in eastern Europe at the expense of the Soviet Union.

Neville Chamberlain – 'guilty man'?

The initial judgements of Neville Chamberlain and the policy of appeasement were extremely negative. Appeasement came to be regarded in the immediate aftermath of the Second World War as a surrender in the face of Hitler's blackmail, rather than a process of mutual agreement. The passionate desire for peace exhibited by Chamberlain in his pursuit of appeasement, so understand-able in itself, came to be viewed as a narrow desire for self-protection which intended to avoid war – at a high moral cost – and, if it came, to try to keep out of fighting on land. The classic denunciation of Chamberlain and appeasement was offered in *Guilty men*, written by a number of left-wing writers including Michael Foot, Frank Owen and Peter Owen (using the collective pseudonym Cato). *Guilty men*, published in 1940, offered a blistering assault on Chamberlain, who was castigated for championing the policy of appeasement during a period when it had very little chance of success. Indeed, *Guilty men* suggests Chamberlain deliberately raised unrealistic hopes among the British public that meek surrender to Hitler's aggressive and bullying territorial demands could bring long-lasting peace and stability to Europe. Overall, *Guilty men* is best described as a politically biased attack on the conduct of British foreign policy in the late 1930s. It portrays appeasement as a combination of calculated deception, incompetent leadership, diplomatic bungling and extremely poor military planning.

When the full horrors of the Nazi death camps were revealed at the end of the Second World War, most people asked why Hitler had not been stopped earlier by the use of military force. Not surprisingly, Chamberlain's drive to appease Hitler was generally viewed with head-hanging shame and deep regret. In fact, a key aspect of the immediate post-war years was the practice of politicians, journalists and historians, with no access to government archives, to pass instant historical judgements on the conduct of foreign policy during the 1930s.

In one of the first post-war historical studies of appeasement, *Munich: prologue to tragedy* (1948), by John Wheeler-Bennett, Chamberlain is stridently criticised for his shortsighted approach to foreign policy during the Czech crisis of 1938. The Munich agreement is described by Wheeler-Bennett as a 'case study in the disease of political myopia which affected the leaders and peoples of Europe in between the wars'. According to Wheeler-Bennett, the policy of appeasement was championed by an ineffective leader, Chamberlain, who completely failed to confront the moral issues inherent in negotiating with an openly aggressive dictator such as Hitler, and to appreciate that war is often preferable to peace bought at a very high moral cost.

In the 1950s and early 1960s, a stream of memoirs from politicians, Foreign Office officials, diplomats, army, navy and air force chiefs and newspaper editors also denounced Chamberlain and the policy of appeasement in equally critical tones. Sir Winston Churchill, the wartime prime minister who led Britain to victory against Nazi Germany, claimed in his memoirs that appeasement, operating from a position of military weakness, as it had under Chamberlain, was doomed to failure. Sir Anthony Eden added further weight to this argument, by claiming in his memoirs that appeasing the dictators was the misguided personal policy of Chamberlain, which was opposed by major figures in the Foreign Office and some leading members of the cabinet.

Modern revisionism

By the mid-1960s, it seemed the judgement of Chamberlain as a 'guilty man', following a cowardly and flawed policy, was unlikely ever to be revised. However, the great turning point in the historical debate on Chamberlain and appeasement came in 1967, when the British government, led by Harold Wilson, allowed access by historians, under the '30-year rule', to key government documents on the foreign policy of the National government of the late 1930s.

What followed was a quite remarkable series of books and articles, which led to a wholesale revision of the orthodox view of Chamberlain and the policy of appeasement. These revisionist historians argued that a concentration on the alleged guilt and incompetence of Chamberlain had obscured a fair-minded analysis of the difficulties facing British policy makers in the 1930s. To them, Chamberlain was a prisoner of a set of circumstances which made a policy of standing up to Hitler impracticable, and one based on securing peace, even at considerable moral cost, preferable to fighting a war in which the odds were heavily stacked against Britain and France. Another key contribution of these revisionists was their portrayal of Chamberlain, not as a weak and incompetent leader, lacking in sound diplomatic judgement, but as a realistic and able politician who realised the danger posed by Hitler, recognised that Britain and France were in no position to keep order in Europe and attempted to do everything possible to avoid war.

The revisionists also suggested that British foreign policy in the 1930s should be analysed within an international context which gives due emphasis to rival ideologies, economic difficulties and social problems. The revisionists claim that British guilt for not stopping Hitler's programme of aggression cannot be pinned on Chamberlain alone. They suggest there were three important reasons why Chamberlain adopted the policy of appeasement:

1 the British economy did not contain enough skilled workers to produce rapid rearmament without severely disrupting the fragile economic recovery from the 'great slump';
2 the army and naval chiefs constantly warned Chamberlain that Britain was not militarily prepared to fight a war against Germany, Italy and Japan simultaneously – and Chamberlain accepted their arguments;
3 public opinion before 1937 opposed all-out rearmament and wished to avoid war.

In the light of these factors, appeasement was a logical policy choice which attempted to persuade Nazi Germany to live in peace with the rest of Europe before accepting that military force had to be used.

David Dilks, one of the leading revisionists, has been at the forefront of the historical rehabilitation of Chamberlain. Dilks suggests the policy of appease-ment grew out of the failure of the 1919 peace settlement to create an effective balance of power in Europe and prevent a resurgence of German military strength. Dilks acknowledges that Chamberlain firmly believed that Germany had a genuine case for a revision of the Treaty of Versailles and also fully understood that the possession of military strength was fundamental to a successful foreign policy. He recognised that Britain lacked sufficient military strength, in the short term at least, to fight Germany. The only sensible policy in such circumstances was to find out whether German grievances could be satisfied without resort to war. Embodied in Chamberlain's pursuit of appeasement was a hope that face-to-face negotiations with Hitler might induce him to solve his grievances by negotiation. This was combined with 'preparing for the worst', which involved Chamberlain spending vast sums on armaments in order to meet force with force if the policy of appeasing Hitler failed.

Chamberlain, as presented by Dilks, is not a deluded politician, but a complex character, possessing a very sharp mind, which weighed up all possibilities before deciding on any course of action. According to Dilks, Chamberlain constantly wrestled with nagging doubts about whether Hitler's aims were limited or vast. Chamberlain wanted peace, not purely for narrow selfish reasons, but because he genuinely did hate the prospect of plunging Britain into a Second World War.

The key aim of Chamberlain's pursuit of appeasement was to revise the Treaty of Versailles, to Hitler's satisfaction, en route to the conclusion of a new general settlement of European problems. But appeasement was not peace at any price. It was based on the underlying premise that if Germany intended to dominate Europe by force then Britain would go to war. Indeed, Dilks argues that if Chamberlain had been simply following a foreign policy which aimed to drive Hitler ever eastward, towards an inevitable settling of accounts with the Soviet Union, with Britain remaining aloof from such a conflict, then there was no sense or need for Chamberlain to offer a guarantee to Poland in March 1939.

As a result of a detailed examination of British government documents, the revisionists have overturned the negative contemporary view of Chamberlain as a 'guilty man' and the policy of appeasement as an act of 'shameful surrender'. It has now become commonplace to view Chamberlain not as a weak and ineffective leader following a morally bankrupt policy, but as a complex and able leader with a clear-sighted approach to foreign policy.

There are some revisionists who suggest that appeasement, rather than aiming at European peace, was a domestic-orientated policy, concerned primarily with Britain's narrowly defined self-interest. According to Maurice Cowling, the policy of appeasement, as operated by Chamberlain, made sense for the Conservative Party because it offered the best hope of retaining the empire and preventing the formation of a wartime coalition with the Labour Party, which at that time was committed to weakening the free market and setting up a costly welfare state. To add strength to this argument, Cowling further contends that an examination of Chamberlain's entire political career reveals an obsession with domestic politics, national self-interest and the electoral fortunes of the Conservative Party. As a result, Cowling suggests domestic considerations were the dominant factor in Chamberlain's decision to champion the policy of appeasement. Indeed, Chamberlain viewed the European crisis as a very unwelcome intrusion on his more pressing concerns about the British economy, the empire and the upcoming general election. For Cowling, Chamberlain's biggest mistake was to abandon the policy, in face of hostile public opinion, after March 1939. He suggests that if the policy of appeasement had continued, even after March 1939, then France would not have been defeated and British cities would not have been bombed during the Battle of Britain. In support of this view, John Charmley has suggested that Britain very nearly bankrupted itself attempting to 'stand alone' against Nazi Germany from May 1940 to June 1941. Even more controversial is the view of Norman Stone, who has argued that the outcome of the Second World War led to eastern Europe being dominated by Stalin, a communist dictator, whose regime was even more brutal and genocidal than Hitler's.

This is, of course, a 'what if' theory rather than a more realistic 'what was possible' theory. Even if Chamberlain had wanted peace at any price, or to have continued with appeasement, he would still have needed to convince a majority of British public opinion, which became impossible as Hitler's brutal attacks on small nations created greater and greater outrage. The British people could never have lived in harmony with, or even tolerated, a Nazi-dominated Europe, and they were quite prepared to bankrupt themselves if that meant living in a Nazi-free Europe.

One of the major problems with the revisionist interpretations is the extent to which they have relied on the official documents of the British government and its leading ministers. The chief danger of relying on such documents is that they were drafted, collected and selected by the people who supported the policy of appeasement. In many cases, the revisionists have provided a justification of why Neville Chamberlain and the British government acted. It is all too easy to believe the path followed by Chamberlain was the only one available, the most logical and the most sensible. What is lacking in many revisionist studies (except for Cowling) is the sense in which appeasement operated within the broader context of political debate inside and outside parliament. An even more glaring omission in most revisionist studies is a detailed discussion of British intelligence reports, which provide a great deal of information about the plans of the Nazi regime. These intelligence reports, which Chamberlain and leading Foreign Office officials read, all pointed to the conclusion that Hitler's aims were not limited to revision of the Treaty of Versailles, but headed on the path of an attempt to dominate Europe by force.

A post-revisionist era?

In more recent times, therefore, a definite counter-reaction to the revisionist school on Chamberlain and appeasement, supported by the present author, and others, is now taking shape. Of course, there have always been critical accounts of Chamberlain and appeasement. Until recently, however, such views tended to lie uncomfortably alongside the more extensive body of revisionist literature.

Yet, even in the midst of the revisionist rehabilitation of Chamberlain, a deeply critical – but important – view of Chamberlain was put forward by Keith Middlemass, whose meticulous research was also based on the official records of the National government. Middlemass defines the policy of appeasement as practised by Chamberlain as a 'diplomacy of illusion'. The major issue for Middlemass is not whether it was immoral to appease Hitler but whether it was advisable to do so when all logical judgement suggested such a policy was certain to fail. According to Middlemass, appeasement failed because of poor timing, a lack of judgement and poor planning. Chamberlain should be criticised because he conducted foreign policy as a one-man band, used the cabinet as lap dogs, muzzled the Foreign Office and fed the public miserly scraps of unrealistic information about the prospects of lasting peace. All of these errors might not have been so crucial if appeasement had been based on a workable defence strategy which bought time in preparation for a future war, but in reality appeasement was underpinned by a defensive strategy which neither protected Britain from air attack nor deterred Hitler from achieving his foreign-policy aims through aggression. Overall, appeasement under Chamberlain was based on the illusion that Hitler's aims were limited merely to a revision of the Treaty of Versailles and could be satisfied by face-to-face negotiations and written agreements.

In more recent times, R. A. C. Parker has produced what he calls a 'counter-revisionist' theory of Chamberlain and appeasement which very skilfully combines elements of the older, critical view of Chamberlain with insights provided by the revisionists. Indeed, Parker has now moved the debate into what can be termed a post-revisionist phase, out of which a new synthesis of Chamberlain and appeasement is starting to take shape. The post-revisionist era is likely to produce a more balanced perspective.

Parker fully accepts the revisionist view of Chamberlain as a competent, able and even clear-sighted politician who had a dominant influence over foreign policy during the late 1930s. However, he rejects, with great skill, the central view of the revisionists, namely that appeasement was dictated by economic and military weakness. On the contrary, Parker suggests that the type of appease-ment followed by Chamberlain was chosen from a range of alternative policies which were skilfully, and all too quickly, rejected, and was pursued with a zeal and obstinacy which clouded Chamberlain's political judgement.

Chamberlain began his mission to appease Hitler with a great deal of cabinet support, but as events unfolded many within the cabinet began to hesitate and to have doubts about the morality and likely success of the policy. However, Chamberlain's supremacy as prime minister was such that he was always able to find some way of manoeuvring his way, with great tactical finesse, free of cabinet restraint to continue with his own preferred course of action. According to Parker, Chamberlain pursued the policy of appeasement with extreme obstinacy, rejecting expert advice and the reasonable suggestions of his critics, and in the process stifled any serious chance of preventing the outbreak of the Second World War.

It seems the historical debate is starting to move towards a more balanced evaluation of appeasement. Many historians are beginning to ask whether the rehabilitation of Chamberlain went too far in the first place, ending up, in some extreme cases, with Chamberlain being portrayed as some sort of far-sighted and visionary leader, when, in the context of the times, appeasement was in fact a very high-risk strategy, fraught with danger, resembling a form of crisis management and lacking in morality. Chamberlain failed to appreciate that constantly yielding to pressure from an aggressive power only delays war, but does not prevent it.

Conclusion

Under Chamberlain, appeasement was not simply a foreign policy which he hoped would succeed, but an obstinate and dogmatic belief system, which saw any other policy as unthinkable. Chamberlain, in spite of Foreign Office advice to the contrary, believed that Hitler could be persuaded to pursue his aims by peaceful means in collaboration with Britain, France and Italy. In the place of expert advice, and the often wise views of his critics, Chamberlain wanted to follow his own views, and surrounded himself with an 'inner circle' of advisers, mostly composed of 'yes men', who endorsed his judgement rather than questioning it. The military strategy which underpinned Chamberlain's diplomacy was also wedded to a long war of self-defence, which took very little account of how the French army, with very limited British support, could hold a resurgent German army, which had developed a new style of 'lightning warfare' (*Blitzkrieg*). In essence, Chamberlain's conduct of appeasement was a crisis management strategy – not a fully worked out foreign policy. It was pursued by a very obstinate leader who saw war as a real possibility and who attempted desperately to prevent it by trying to encourage Hitler to solve his grievances by peaceful negotiation. It failed because Hitler continued on the path he had chosen for himself, a path which had no place for the policy of appeasement. It should also be emphasised that a very high level of news management and media manipulation (now called 'spin doctoring') was employed by Chamberlain in order to foster the view that appeasement was extremely popular with the general public. In fact, the foreign policy which Chamberlain rejected and constantly undermined, namely collective security through the League of Nations, was by far the most popular one with the British public. After the occupation of Czechoslovakia in March 1939, the most popular policy among the public was for Britain to gain an alliance with the Soviet Union, but Chamberlain opted instead for a dubious guarantee to Poland. An opinion poll, taken in July 1939, showed that 84 per cent of the public favoured a Soviet alliance, while the highest opinion poll rating for appeasement was 51 per cent (taken on the day the Munich agreement was signed).

It cannot be denied that political judgements – especially the wrong ones taken by Chamberlain from 1937 onwards – played a deeply significant part in the outbreak of the Second World War. Appeasement failed because Chamberlain took much too long to accept that Hitler could not be appeased and therefore a different policy, one which took military steps to deter or stop his aggression, was the only sensible way to deal with him. Chamberlain's worst error was to believe he could march Hitler on the yellow brick road to peace when in reality Hitler was marching very firmly on the road to war.

Select bibliography

There are numerous books on the roles played by Adolf Hitler and Neville Chamberlain in the origins of the Second World War. The following list contains a brief selection of important studies.

Original documents

There are several major document collections relevant to the origins of the Second World War. These feature many key documents relating to British and German foreign policy. The most important are: N. Baynes (ed.), *The speeches of Adolf Hitler*, 2 vols, Oxford, 1942; *Documents on British foreign policy*, 2nd series, vols 1–19, 3rd series, vols 1–9, London, 1946–82; *Documents on German foreign policy*, series C, vols 1–6, series D, vols 1–13, London, 1949–82; J. Granville, *The major international treaties, 1914–73*, London, 1974.

The origins of the Second World War – introductory and general studies

There are many useful introductory books which examine the origins of the Second World War, all of which include lengthy discussions of Hitler's foreign policy and Neville Chamberlain's pursuit of appeasement. The most useful of these are: A. Adamthwaite, *The making of the Second World War*, 2nd edn, London, 1979; P. Bell, *The origins of the Second World War in Europe*, 2nd edn, London, 1997; R. Henig, *The origins of the Second World War 1933–1939*, London, 1985; R. Overy, *The origins of the Second World War*, London, 1987; E. Robertson (ed.), *The origins of the Second World War*, London, 1971; A. J. P. Taylor, *The origins of the Second World War*, London, 1961.

Biographies of Hitler

There are many important biographies of Adolf Hitler, most notably: A. Bullock, *Hitler. A study in tyranny*, revised edn, London, 1964; J. Fest, *Hitler*, London, 1974; I. Kershaw, *Hitler*, 2 vols, London, 1998, 2000; N. Stone, *Hitler*, London, 1980; J. Toland, *Adolf Hitler*, New York, 1976.

Hitler and foreign policy

There are a vast number of studies of Hitler's foreign policy and its role in the origins of the Second World War, including: W. Carr, *Arms, autarchy and aggression. A study in German foreign policy*, 2nd edn, London, 1979; K. Hildebrand, *The foreign policy of the Third Reich*, London, 1973; N. Rich, *Hitler's war aims*, 2 vols, London, 1973, 1974; G. Weinberg, *The foreign policy of Hitler's Germany: Starting World War 2*, London, 1980.

Neville Chamberlain and the policy of appeasement

There are several important studies of Neville Chamberlain and the policy of appeasement, most notably: D. Dutton, *Neville Chamberlain*, London, 2001; K. Feiling, *The life of Neville Chamberlain*, London, 1946; L. Fuchser, *Neville Chamberlain and appeasement. A study in the politics of history*, London, 1982; H. Hyde, *Neville Chamberlain*, London, 1976; F. McDonough, *Neville Chamberlain, appeasement and the British road to war*, Manchester, 1998; K. Middlemass, *The diplomacy of illusion. The British government and Germany, 1937–1939*, London, 1972; R. A. C. Parker, *Chamberlain and appeasement. British policy and the coming of the Second World War*, London, 1993.

Key events

Several useful studies cover the key events leading to the Second World War. For the Abyssinian affair, see F. Hardie, *The Abyssinian crisis*, London, 1974. For the Rhineland crisis, see J. Emmerson, *The Rhineland crisis*, London, 1977. For the Czech crisis and the Munich agreement, see K. Robbins, *Munich 1938*, London, 1968. For the British guarantee to Poland, see S. Newman, *March 1939. The British guarantee to Poland*, Oxford, 1976. For the failure of the Anglo-Soviet alliance negotiations, see R. Manne, 'The Foreign Office and the failure of the Anglo-Soviet rapprochement', *Journal of Contemporary History* (1981).

Chronology

1918 *11 November:* German representatives sign the armistice which ends the 'Great War'.

1919 *19 January:* The Paris peace conference opens.

February: The League of Nations is established.

28 June: The Treaty of Versailles is signed by the German government, under protest.

1922 *16 April:* Germany and the Soviet Union sign the Treaty of Rapallo.

1923 *January:* French troops occupy the Ruhr industrial region of Germany in order to enforce the payment of reparations by the German government.

1924 *April:* The Dawes Plan is introduced. This US-inspired economic aid package offers loans to Germany and leads to the resumption of reparations payments.

1925 *October:* The Locarno treaties are signed. The treaties are regarded as a major act of reconciliation between Germany and the Allied nations.

1926 *September:* Germany joins the League of Nations.

1928 *August:* The Kellogg–Briand pact is signed. This pledge to 'renounce war' is eventually signed by 56 nations.

1929 *October:* The Wall Street stock market crash in the USA ignites the worst economic depression of the twentieth century.

1931 *September:* Japan occupies Manchuria (north-east China).

1932 The World Disarmament Conference opens (but eventually ends in failure).

1933 *30 January:* Adolf Hitler is appointed German chancellor.

14 October: Germany withdraws from the League of Nations and the World Disarmament Conference.

1934 *26 January:* Germany signs a non-aggression pact with Poland.

25 July: Dollfuss is assassinated in an abortive Nazi coup in Austria. Hitler denies involvement.

2 August: President Hindenburg dies. Hitler declares himself Führer of the German people. The German army swears a personal oath of loyalty to Hitler.

1935 *16 March:* Conscription is introduced in Germany and rearmament is announced.

11–14 April: Stresa conference: Britain, France and Italy denounce the German decision to rearm.

2 May: France signs a treaty of mutual assistance with the Soviet Union.

18 June: Anglo-German naval agreement is signed.

October: Italy invades Abyssinia.

1936 *7 March:* German troops occupy the demilitarised Rhineland in violation of the Locarno treaties.

9 September: The Four Year Plan is announced in Germany.

25 October: The Rome–Berlin Axis is signed.

October: Spanish Civil War breaks out.

1936 *25 November:* The Anti-Comintern pact between Germany and Japan is signed (Italy joins on 6 November 1937).

1937 *28 May:* Neville Chamberlain becomes British prime minister, firmly committed to a policy of appeasement.

5 November: Hitler announces his future war plans to leading service chiefs and foreign minister (Hossbach memorandum).

19 November: Lord Halifax meets Hitler in order to improve Anglo-German relations.

1938 *4 February:* Blomberg, war minister, and Fritsch, army commander in chief, are both dismissed. Hitler becomes supreme commander of the armed forces.

20 February: Anthony Eden resigns as British foreign secretary.

12 March: German troops march into Austria.

13 March: The *Anschluss* (Austria's union with Germany) is officially declared.

24 April: Konrad Henlein, leader of the Czechoslovak Sudeten German Party, demands 'autonomy' for the Sudeten area of Czechoslovakia.

20 May: The 'May crisis'. Britain, France and the Soviet Union warn Hitler of the consequences of an unprovoked German attack on Czechoslovakia.

30 May: Hitler gives a directive to the German army for 'the destruction of Czechoslovakia', set for 1 October 1938.

15 September: Chamberlain flies to Germany to meet Hitler at Berchtesgaden to solve the Sudeten crisis.

22 September: Chamberlain meets Hitler at Bad Godesberg. The talks end with no settlement.

29 September: Munich conference: Germany, Britain, Italy and France agree to Sudetenland being incorporated into Nazi Germany.

30 September: The Munich agreement is signed. Chamberlain declares it is 'peace in our time' on his return to 10 Downing Street.

9 November: *Kristallnacht* ('night of broken glass'), a night of organised attacks against Jews in Germany.

1939 *15 March:* German troops occupy Czechoslovakia.

21 March: Hitler demands the return of Danzig from Poland.

31 March: Britain and France offer guarantee to Poland.

22 May: The 'Pact of Steel' is signed between Germany and Italy.

23 August: The Nazi–Soviet pact is signed.

1 September: Germany invades Poland.

3 September: Britain and France declare war on Germany.

Index

Index

Germany: Berlin Olympic Games (1936), 26;
economy, 4, 12–13, 32; and the First World
War, 1, 7; Four Year Plan (1936), 25–6, 28;
Halifax visit to, 45–6; and the Locarno treaties,
10–11; *Luftwaffe*, 25; rearmament, 19, 21–2, 26;
reparations payments by, 7, 8, 9–10, 13–14;
and the Spanish Civil War, 25; and
Stresemann's foreign policy, 10–11, 11–12;
territorial expansion of Nazi Germany, 66; and
the Treaty of Versailles (1919), 4, 5–8, 9, 12,
14–15, 18, 32; Weimar Republic, 9, 13, 13–14,
20; *see also* Hitler, Adolf
Great Depression, 12–13, 32, 43

Halifax, Lord, 45–6, 55, 62, 69
Henderson, Sir Neville, 44
Hindenburg, Paul von, 13
Hitler, Adolf, 13, 15, 17, 18; and the Anglo-French
guarantee to Poland, 67; and Anglo-German
relations, 19, 26–7, 29; and *Anschluss* with
Germany, 20, 48–9; and appeasement, 44,
45–6, 48, 86; and the Czech crisis, 50–2, 57,
58; foreign policy aims and actions, 1, 17–30,
40, 64, 73, 77–8, 79–80; and the Hossbach
meeting, 46, 47; and the Munich agreement,
52, 53–4, 62, 63, 64; and the Nazi–Soviet pact,
69–71; occupation of Czechoslovakia, 63,
64–5, 73–4; and the outbreak of war, 71–3, 74,
75, 78, 79–80; revisionist view of, 78, 79–80;
and the Rhineland crisis (1936), 24–5, 32, 80;
see also Germany
Hoare–Laval pact, 23–4
Hossbach memorandum (1937), 29, 46

intentionalist view of Hitler's foreign-policy aims,
78
Italy, 21, 25, 33; Chamberlain's visit to, 63–4;
invasion of Abyssinia, 22–4, 38

Japan, 12, 26, 38
Jews, Nazi brutality against, 63

Kellogg–Briand pact (1928), 11
Keynes, John Maynard, 4, 32

Lausanne conference (1932), 13–14
Laval, Pierre, 23
League of Nations, 7, 8, 22, 48, 65, 69; British
public attitudes to, 31, 36; and collective
security, 8, 36, 38, 39, 86; German withdrawal
from, 19; and Italian invasion of Abyssinia, 23;
and Japanese invasion of Manchuria, 12
Lloyd George, David, 4, 5, 9, 14, 31, 43
Locarno treaties, 10–11, 13, 24, 43
Luftwaffe, 25
Lytton, Lord, 12

MacDonald, Ramsay, 12, 16, 19
Manchuria, Japanese invasion of, 12, 38
Mass-Observation poll on appeasement, 62
Mosley, Sir Oswald, 37

Munich agreement (1938), 1, 34, 52–5, 58–9, 64;
critics of, 61–2, 81; public reaction to, 62
Mussolini, Benito, 13, 21, 26, 33, 44, 47, 48, 49, 55;
and the Anglo-French guarantee to Poland, 67;
and British appeasement, 63–4; and the Munich
agreement, 52; and Nazi invasion of Poland, 72

navy, British Royal Navy, 34
newspapers, support for appeasement, 36, 40
Nuremberg trials, 1, 77

pacifist groups and appeasement, 37
Papen, Franz von, 14
Paris peace conference (1919), 3, 4–8, 15
Poincaré, Raymond, 10
Poland, 5, 7, 20; Anglo-French guarantee to,
65–7, 71, 74, 79, 80, 86; German invasion of
(1939), 1, 71–3, 75

Rapallo, Treaty of (1922), 18
revisionist historians, 1, 78–80, 81–4
Rhineland crisis (1936), 24–5, 32, 80
Ribbentrop, Joachim von, 26–7, 29, 47
Romania, 5
Roosevelt, Franklin D., 44, 47
Ruhr, French occupation of, 10
Runciman, Lord, 50

Schuschnigg, Kurt von, 48–9
Second World War outbreak, 1, 71–3, 75–6, 86;
Hitlocentric interpretation of, 77–8; post-
revisionist views on, 85; revisionist views on,
78–80, 83–4
Soviet Union, 5, 22, 33; communist views of
fascism, 40–1; and Czechoslovakia, 50, 51;
failure of Anglo-French–Soviet agreement, 65,
68–9, 70–1, 79, 86; and Hitler's foreign policy,
17, 18–19; and the League of Nations, 31; and
the Locarno treaties, 11; Nazi–Soviet pact (1939),
54, 69–71; and the Spanish Civil War, 25
Spanish Civil War, 25, 44
Stalin, Joseph, 13, 54, 84; and the Nazi–Soviet
pact, 69–71
Stresa Front, 21–2
Stresemann, Gustav, 10–11, 11–12

unemployment in Britain, 32
United States, 34, 44; Wall Street crash (1929),
12, 32

Vansittart, Robert, 47
Versailles Treaty (1919), 3, 5–9, 12, 14–15, 16, 18,
21; and the Anglo-German naval agreement,
22; and appeasement, 32, 38, 44, 82, 83, 85;
and the Rhineland crisis, 24, 25
Vienna, Congress of (1814–15), 7

Wilson, Sir Horace, 47, 58
World Disarmament Conference, 14, 19

Yugoslavia, and national self-determination, 5